{SPEAKING OF MISSION}
VOLUME 2

OTHER BOOKS IN THIS SERIES

Speaking of Mission

First published in 2006, Volume 1 in this series includes the lectures of eight scholars who reimagine global mission for our time. Speaking of Mission addresses a breadth of mission issues through biblical analysis and reflections on contemporary practice. These issues include how to mobilise local churches in global mission, the nature of missional leadership, evangelism, social justice and cultural development, the role of the Holy Spirit, and the holiness of God as an impetus for mission.

Morling Press

Speaking of Mission Volume 2

First Published 2013

120 Herring Rd Macquarie Park NSW 2113 Australia

Phone: +61 2 9878 0201

Email: enquiries@morling.edu.au

www.morlingcollege.com

© **Morling Press 2013**

This publication is copyright. Other than for the purposes of study and subject to the conditions of the Copyright Act, no part of it in any form or by any means (electronic, mechanical, micro-copying, photocopying or otherwise) may be reproduced, stored in a retrieval system or transmitted without the permission of the publisher.

ISBN: 978-0-9922755-0-1

Designed by Beni Creative **www.benicreative.com.au**

CONTENTS

Introduction vii
DARRELL JACKSON

1 The Practice of Placed Mission 9
MICHAEL FROST

2 Mission After Christendom 21
STUART MURRAY WILLIAMS

3 Fitting into the Triune God's Missional Plot 33
MARY FISHER

4 Following Jesus into Suburbia 49
SIMON CAREY HOLT

5 Lost in Salvation 65
MICHAEL DUNCAN

6 How Dirty Are the Hands and Feet that Follow Jesus 81
JON OWEN

7 Everyday Theology in the iWorld 93
JUSTINE TOH

8 Preaching to the Birds? 107
MICK POPE

Contributors 121

Endnotes 123

INTRODUCTION

This slim volume showcases a dazzling array of missional wisdom and experience, and I'm thrilled to be writing the introduction. If nothing else, it's allowed me a sneak preview of a diverse collection of literary and missiological gems. More than that, however, the range of authors and the themes they address have re-affirmed my sense of call as a missiologist. I repeatedly found myself thinking "This is why I do what I do!"

It's never an easy task to introduce a set of collected works and I was determined from the outset to avoid offering a literary trailer to each of the chapters. In the 2006 romantic comedy, *The Holiday*, the character played by Cameron Diaz directs a company producing voiceovers for Hollywood movie trailers. The comedic aspect is that we, the audience, overhear her imagined trailers, *basso profundo*, summarising the dramatic moments of her life. In the movie we see her trying to break free of this tendency in order to make real connections with the people around her. Each of the chapters in this collection makes its own highly creative connections to the realities of life faced by their respective authors. I discovered that each, in its own way, was engaging and transforming the way we might otherwise view such realities. In the face of this fact, it was immediately apparent that an attempt on my part to summarise each chapter would result in a dull and lifeless introduction. The colours and melodies of each chapter contribute to an artistic and theological whole that reflects a surprising harmony of purpose, and so I've set out to try to create a literary impression of what I've seen (as well as read) in these chapters.

So, what kind of introduction is this? It might be unusual, but attempting to review the chapters took me back in my memories to the small fishing village in which I grew up. My dad spent a few seasons working the trawlers. I vividly recall the fleet of trawlers making its way back to harbour, trailed by an aerial plume of seagulls eager for the discarded waste. As the gulls touched down on the quayside to form small groups I would run at them, delighted to see them scatter and take to the skies, wheeling and dipping, calling angrily, and waiting their chance to return to the landing site. Seagulls have that tendency. Run at them and they scatter in all directions, with little or no semblance of moving in concert. One of the few occasions when gulls move together is when they collectively trail a fishing boat or passenger ferry, in the expectation of a tasty reward. I've also come to realise that gulls will do that for many hours, even days. They have remarkable endurance.

Had I taken a metaphorical run at the chapters in this volume I might have expected them, on first glance, to scatter in all directions. What connections might one possibly draw between, for example, robustly eccentric accounts of the *ordo salutis*, the built environment, the iWorld, or eco-missiology? It appears that what we have here is a collection of theological seagulls — with little or no likelihood of murmuration (Google it!). Or so it might seem.

A more careful reading of the chapters, however, reveals a small number of tightly interrelated themes. What I see here illustrates the missional, incarnational, relational and ecological concerns that lie at the heart of Michael Frost's enduring vision for the Tinsley Institute. Together, these help to explain why this Institute is such a stimulating place to work. As with the flock of gulls trailing in the wake of the fishing boat, these concerns motivate endurance in the face of the long haul that is the task of re-purposing missiology for each and every new challenge it encounters. Our authors argue that the Christian faith and its theological traditions provide an adequate and coherent response to the questions posed by the contemporary iWorld; offer resources in the seemingly overwhelming struggle with climate change; require us to bind the wounds of those alienated by the urban environment; provide a framework for interpreting the social spaces in which we live and work; and, ultimately, suggest that in committing to such things we become participants in the creative, salvific and missional purposes of a triune God, the *missio Dei trinitatis*.

What strikes me about these authors is the manner in which they are wrestling with realities that resonate deeply for many of us. I too frequently hear students talk about "life in the real world", by which they mean life beyond the campus of colleges such as Morling. I understand what they are trying to say and sympathise to some extent with their desire to remain rooted in the communities that they are serving in the name of Jesus. I can hardly take issue with them in this regard: identification with the world that we serve is rooted in an incarnational vision of the world.

What I choose to take issue with is the way in which my students too readily assume that what they encounter beyond the campus is "real". What our authors have done here is help us to understand that what is encountered there is frequently a distorted, even obscured, version of what God considers "real". A biblical worldview involves an understanding that God's version of reality is "more real" than the reality encountered in the mundane affairs of a fallen humanity.

The perceptions of a minister working in the midst of urban deprivation are certainly "real". A student frustrated with a congregation that struggles to kick the habits of Christendom is experiencing something "real". A Pacific Islander working hard to keep his home above rising sea-levels is very aware that his problems are "real". These are hardly contestable facts, but despite this, I want to argue that they are not ultimate realities.

That is why our authors not only wrestle with the issues that concern them both personally and professionally, but it also explains why they write in a way that envisions the future which God intends for a restored humanity. What drives these authors to write, I suspect, is a shared conviction that ultimate reality is rooted in the activity and character of a personal, purposive and goal-oriented God, revealed to us in Jesus the Messiah. Furthermore, that reality is given expression in the conviction that God's missional purpose is to extend his authority over the whole of the created order. Ultimate reality is glimpsed, and occasionally experienced, with the irruption of God's coming reign into the world that our authors are writing about and of which they are a part.

I'm left in no doubt by this collection of annual Tinsley lectures that the real world is right at the heart of the concerns of a college like Morling. I wholeheartedly commend them to you.

DARRELL JACKSON

Feast day of St Desideratus, May 2013

Chapter One

THE PRACTICE OF PLACED MISSION

MICHAEL FROST

It's easier to love humanity than to love your neighbour — Eric Hoffer

A Tale of Two Cities

One year, after a hectic speaking schedule in Phnom Penh, Cambodia, I happened to have the day off alone on my birthday. At first I didn't mind that idea. I thought I'd sleep in a little longer than usual, take a leisurely breakfast by the pool in my cheap hotel, wander down the street to the city's famous Central Market to buy a gift for my wife, and then meander carelessly around the teaming streets, taking in the sights and sounds of this fascinating city. Wrong. Sleeping in and breakfasting by the pool worked out, but everything else was a disaster. You see, Phnom Penh is not a city for pedestrians. Not only are the roads clogged with bikes, trucks and cars, the sidewalks are littered with hawkers, food carts and motorbikes. In fact, the sidewalks themselves are cracked and broken due to the excessive use of cars and bikes parking on them illegally. Walking through Phnom Penh in the heat of the day, trying to avoid tripping over or being run down or knocked over requires maximum attention. Strolling, meandering or wandering was out of the question. Just getting to and from the Central Market was an exhausting enterprise, not to mention how overwhelming it was to be harassed and bustled by the stallholders all pressing me to buy their wares. Even before lunch, I had stumbled back to my tiny air-conditioned hotel room defeated by the city. I tried again that afternoon, hoping to get down to the banks of the Tonle Sap River for a stroll along the promenade, but I was driven back by the bustle and the heat. I ended up spending a depressing day in my dingy hotel room on my birthday.

In Phnom Penh the motorbike is everything. Without one you're trapped in a very small part of your environment. In this way, the built environment shapes the residents' sense of community and wellbeing. But is it much different in Western cities? Well, it looks very different at first glance, but it isn't much different in reality. I was once the guest of some friends-of-a-friend in Thousand Oaks, in the north-western part of the Greater Los Angeles Area. Thousand Oaks has been named one of the "Best Places to Live" by some investment magazines. Situated in the Conejo Valley in Ventura County, and featuring, you guessed it, an abundance of Californian oak trees, it is a typical American suburban community with well manicured lawns and neat houses arranged in cul-de-sacs. I once spent a free day in this city as well and, surprisingly, I had a very similar experience to my birthday in Phnom Penh.

Initially I thought I would stroll to the downtown area and get some lunch and take in the sights, but my hosts informed me that Thousand Oaks has no downtown. It was part of a master-planned city created by the Janss Investment Company in the mid-1950s, which included about 3,000 dwellings built around the Janss Marketplace shopping mall. Since then several other malls and many other residences have popped up. Okay, I conceded, I'll walk down to the mall then. No, I was informed, that would be impossible. For a start none of the streets in the area where I was staying has sidewalks and, secondly, to get to the mall from the house required crossing an interstate freeway, which was impossible on foot. Indeed, it was thought if the neighbours saw a strange man wandering the empty streets of their community it would arouse great suspicion. My hosts were heading out to work for the day, taking both the cars, so I was effectively trapped in the house. It was a very comfortable house and my hosts were very generous, but in reality I was as stuck in their palatial house as I was in that cheap hotel in Phnom Penh. In both cases I resorted to the Internet to check email and social media.

Our cities seem to be designed, for different reasons, to keep us from incarnational connection. This was the very thing Jane Jacobs was alerting us to a generation ago when she rather colourfully described what housing developers have given us as,

> [l]ow income projects that become worse centers of delinquency, vandalism, and general social hopelessness than the slums they were supposed to replace; middle income housing projects which are truly marvels of dullness and regimentation, sealed against any buoyancy or vitality of city life; luxury housing projects that mitigate their inanity with a vapid vulgarity; cultural centers that are unable to support a good bookstore; civic centers that are avoided by everyone but bums, who have fewer choices of loitering than others; commercial centers that are lacklustre imitations of standardized suburban chain store shopping; promenades that go from no place to nowhere and have no promenaders; expressways that eviscerate great cities. This is not the rebuilding of cities, *this is the sacking of cities*.[1] [Italics added]

Of course, housing developments and city planning are driven entirely by commercial interests. Their "sacking of the city" is to their gain. Those who make decisions about both our built environment and our electronic environment are not interested in community, justice, amenity or just plain neighbourliness. They're just trying to make a buck. And as a result, we live in neighbourhoods which are simply unwalkable. We allow builders to create houses with facades that look like fortresses, with all the family life tucked away in the rear and surrounded by walls so high no one can see in. We live, glued to our screens, playing games, checking social media, interacting in the flattened, fragmented world of the Internet. We have happily acquiesced to the architects of modern secular living and allowed them to shape our environment according to whatever will make them the biggest return. And none of these planners or builders will ever have to live with the consequences of the cities and neighbourhoods they create. As theologian Jurgen Moltmann concludes, "Predatory exploitation is practised only by alien and homeless groups of people."[2] Interestingly, the protected lives of those who live in gated communities and walled houses is pleasant but inhumane due to the lack of human closeness and community, while the unprotected life of the slums has far greater potential for a truly humane community. Living in a poor urban neighbourhood might bring certain dangers, but raising children in a suburban estate brings its own dangers. It's just that we don't rate being raised as a self-centred, egotistic consumer as all that dangerous.

Community in the Built Environment

In the face of this relentless sense of *dis*-placement, Tim Gorringe, in his book, *A Theology of the Built Environment*, explores six dimensions of the church to which we must ever hold fast.[3] Indeed, it is as we embrace these six dimensions we provide hope to our defleshed, displaced world that there is another way that human beings can live together. Those six dimensions are:

Firstly, the church is a *local* community, globally networked. In the face of what has been called the "shapeless giantism" of the great cities, people are yearning for, and discovering, the value and necessity of the neighbourhood. The kids of the baby-boom generation who gave us Thousand Oaks want a greater sense of place, community, neighbourliness. Interestingly, Gorringe points out that as long ago as the 1930s, American town planner Clarence Perry was recommending that a neighbourhood should be "small enough for everything to be within walking distance, but large enough to support an elementary school, local stores and services."[4] In their book, *Greening the Built Environment*, the authors recommend a neighbourhood should have "streets laid out on rectangular grids to provide maximum connectivity, and the slowing down of traffic to enable people of diverse backgrounds to meet frequently, informally and for different purposes."[5] Compare this to the current preference for cul-de-sacs, major thoroughfares and freeways. Today, people live in one neighbourhood, work in another, and play in yet another. However, it is also true that the micro politics of education, health, transport and even street design remains obstinately local. And, as Gorringe points out, the importance of the local remains especially obvious for children, the elderly and the disabled. Churches must take this challenge seriously and see themselves as a localizing agency within a neighbourhood, throwing their halls open for community use, funding local initiatives and enterprises, supporting local businesses, praying for their neighbours. The opportunities for the church to be like salt and light in this respect are considerable.

Secondly, the church lives by *memory and tradition*. At a time when church tradition is being dismissed by everyone, including the church itself, Gorringe makes the valuable point that in many communities it is the church which offers the deepest roots. He refers to the cathedral cities in the United Kingdom and the way the churches in those places anchor communities in a shared belief system, a common history and set of values. This hardly relates to our suburban neighbourhoods, but it is nonetheless usually true to say that often the local church in suburban neighbourhoods is the most permanent thing in town. Where businesses come and go, very few other agencies stick it out through thick and thin. The church is one.

Sometimes, we look at a small church comprised of mainly elderly folks and wonder what impact such a group could have. But it is helpful to think that this community of faith forms a repository of old wisdom, memory and long-term shared practice. These are extremely valuable resources in a time of displacement, if only the church could figure out how to share them with their neighbours. I think it was Simone Weil who said that human beings do not survive without roots, and I believe she is right. Sociologists claim that long-time residents make a disproportionately large contribution to a community. But compare this to the highly mobile society in which many of us live. Apparently, on average we live in one place for five years, a statistic that applies to Christians and the clergy as much as to anyone. I believe Christians should be the most rooted people in our community, their loyalty and devotion to a particular geographical area and everyone who lives there should be legendary. I live in the neighbourhood in which I grew up. I have deep, long-term connections with the place and with the community. I went to school with the head of the local chamber of commerce. I share in the history of our village, knowing what problems it has overcome (ocean pollution, high-rise development) and what vexing struggles it avoids addressing (affordable housing, alcohol-related crime). And I drastically limit the amount of travel I do to ensure that my primary energy goes into the local.

Thirdly, the church is a community where *sin is recognised and forgiveness asked for*. In an interesting take on the church's contribution to community, Gorringe argues that we have much to offer if we rediscover our central tenets of confession, repentance and forgiveness. When practised well they foster a faith community of acceptance, hospitality and grace, a community which fights graciously, acknowledges all and is nourished by every contribution. Gorringe says, "A community which lives by sin and forgiveness is not a community of consensus, but a community which has found a way of coping with conflict and difference."[6] In a day and age when sociologists are crying out for ways for communities to practise tolerance, acceptance and grace, the church ought to be a microcosm of these very things. Indeed, surely the only way for these values to be inculcated in a neighbourhood is for face-to-face negotiation to take place and no agency in society seems ready or prepared to broker such discussions. Why not the church? Gorringe again:

> ...the task of the church in plural societies is to both support and radically criticize the framework which holds a plural society together, but also to be an active protagonist for minority-group positions... Without this, community degenerates into communalism, in which community is pitted against community.[7]

How often have you heard stories of churches in conflict with their neighbours or with city planners? How often has the church degenerated into communalism and contributed to social breakdown, rather than offering themselves as brokers in the development of better cities? Churches should take social issues head on. We should practise peace-making and offer our services to the neighbourhood. We should be the "experts" on confession and forgiveness, teaching our community a better way forward, aiding our neighbours to become more tolerant, hospitable and welcoming. At a time when our cities are calling for greater "tolerance" toward others, the church can show what moving beyond mere "tolerance" looks like. "Tolerance" is one of the watchwords of a liberal society, but it is essentially passive.

Christians understand that the proper response to the stranger is more proactive — it is expressed in the biblical practice of "hospitality". Tolerance is the response of the powerful to the less powerful. It carries no imperative to actively help those who are vulnerable, whereas hospitality calls us to enter into relationship with those who are different.

Fourthly, *justice* is essential to community. It seems patently wrong that some of the residents in our cities live in slums or bleak housing estates while others live in mansions in gated communities. The church's contribution to the place in which it finds itself is to contribute continually to this ideal, holding the city to their belief in the equal treatment of equals, and offering practical assistance to those left behind in the rush toward wealth creation. As the former Archbishop of Canterbury, Rowan Williams, says,

> The Church exists to connect people at the level of their hunger for a new world… this is how the Church makes neighbours — not so much by struggling to find ideas that unite us, not even by struggling to make us like each other, but by giving us a role to play, the role of people all equally eager to be fed by one life-giving food.[8]

Fifthly, the church is committed to a *common purpose*, their shared final ends. The universal church is called together by a common story and bound together by a common hope. In this respect, we are indeed a "purpose-driven" people — with apologies to Rick Warren. In being formed distinctly and uniquely by our shared hope in the future promised by God, we know how to be resolutely future-oriented. The Spirit of God is calling us on this journey both as pilgrims (we are shaped by a narrative of where we are going and a sense of how to go on that journey) but also as wayfarers (we're leaving a place that has been familiar, where we mastered the practices of being church but now travel in *terra incognito* with a sense of loss and disorientation). The way for such pilgrims/wayfarers is a journey of mutuality and respect among strangers in our local communities, without pre-determined solutions or formulas; we will need to experiment and discern. This, says Gorringe, is a skill sorely needed by our broader communities. He quotes Kevin Lynch's 1960 book, *The Image of City*, saying that the city landscape should express the common hopes and pleasures of ordinary people, so that "the sense of community may be made flesh."[9] Lynch continued, "Above all, if the environment is visibly organized and sharply identified, then it will become a *place*, remarkable and unmistakable."[10] In other words, in order for the city to survive as a viable public space it must be able to articulate its genuinely common hopes and pleasures. And who will broker the negotiation of what those hopes and pleasures are? Why couldn't it be the church? As it happens, in my city it was the trade union movement that brokered an alliance of concerned residents to discuss ways to foster a more socially just, safe and compassionate place. Called the Sydney Alliance, their stated goal was to bring together diverse community organisations, unions and religious organisations to advance the common good and achieve a fair, just and sustainable city. Their website says, "We do this by providing opportunities for people to have a say in decisions that affect them, their families and everyone working and living in Sydney."[11] Admittedly, some churches have agreed to participate, but it's disappointing that churches aren't at the forefront of catalysing such conversations around the world. Gorringe says,

To the objection that this is too abstract a thing for people to commit themselves to, the answer is that what we are talking about is the sharing and safeguarding of the basic resources of life, and there is nothing more concrete than this.[12]

Sixthly, the church is *semper reformanda*, always in the process of re-creation and rediscovery. Having earlier reminded us of the value of memory and tradition, Gorringe also points out, "[t]hough we are committed to the attempt to construct community this will always be fragile, always in need of re-invention."[13] And so it should be, with each generation of Christ-followers committed to new, fresh expressions of what our place could be like. It keeps us from maintaining some dull status quo, and from our fear of failure in our attempts at experimentation. In the United Kingdom there is a growing awareness of the role churches can play in urban renewal. The Church of England Commission on Urban Life and Faith recently reported on the way government perceives the contribution of religious communities to such regeneration:

> However, as far as the Government is concerned, religion (however sketchily that is perceived) still remains among the most significant elements of civil society and community mobilization. And, as a Commission, we have also heard time and again how shared service within local communities has given rise to opportunities for inter-faith dialogue and common purpose — and of the new opportunities these present for a united witness for the good of the city. These seem to us to focus around three themes:
>
> - The renewed commitment to regeneration and neighbourhood renewal that is coming from many quarters;
> - The intriguing use of language of human flourishing and spirituality in the hopes and visions for what makes a good city;
> - The challenge to celebrate and support the many sources and expressions of faith which are taking place in the city.[14]

Bearing all that in mind, what are the implications of this for Christians wishing to countermand the excarnational impulses that pull us up and out of our neighbourhoods? How can we go down and deep into the cities and villages in which God has placed us? Let's think of Gorringe's six dimensions in terms of innovation. How can we adopt the posture, thinking, behaviour and practices of an incarnational one to engage our communities meaningfully and for God's glory? I'd like to make four simple suggestions:

1. *Anthropologically* (Move in with them): What can we do to become more embedded in our communities, to appreciate their needs, hopes and yearnings? Moving into the neighbourhood is essential. Can you imagine marrying your spouse, then choosing to live separately? It is so common a thing these days for Christians to attend churches several neighbourhoods away that raising the question seems strangely redundant. But I continue to raise it. What sense does it make for all the Christians

to be getting into gas-guzzling 4WD's every Sunday morning and criss-crossing their greater metro regions to go to a church in some distant community? Compare this with a recent article entitled, *Most Americans Want a Walkable Neighborhood, Not a Big House*, which highlights the changing mentality of Americans. It says, "Six in 10 people also said they would sacrifice a bigger house to live in a neighborhood that featured a mix of houses, stores, and businesses within an easy walk."[15] Why wouldn't the church want to lead the way in modelling what this could look like? It's heartening to hear of the Walkable Church movement, a network of church leaders who are trying to promote walkability as a core church value. One of its proponents, Sean Benesh, leads a church in Portland called the Ion Community. He says, "Out of the 5 core values that identify the Ion Community, one of them is related solely to transportation. I believe that if there is one value that could potentially set the Ion Community apart from many churches it is this value: Walkable."[16] Being able to walk to church isn't some magical missional practice, but it does ensure that congregations will be an enfleshed presence in their immediate community. At the very least, pastors should aim to live and serve in the same neighbourhood as their church is in. I am often surprised to hear church leaders ask me whether it matters where they live. But what did Jesus do? He was called Immanuel — "God with us" — and he chose to make "his home among us". We mirror his character in this world when we move in and embrace solidarity with the place to which God has sent us. Kathleen Norris writes, "To be an American is to move on, as if we could outrun change. To attach oneself to place is to surrender to it, and suffer with it."[17]

2. *Empathically* (Listen to them): How can I increase my opportunities to converse with, and listen to, the people I am trying to serve? Listen to them. Can you imagine a doctor prescribing a plan of care without asking questions or conducting examinations? René Laennec, the inventor of the stethoscope, famously said, "Listen to your patients, they are telling you how to heal them". In *The Secular Age*, Charles Taylor questions what occurred between 1500 and 2000 — the modern age of Western society — when in 2000 it was possible not to believe in God, while in 1500 it was impossible to do so. His answer: disenchantment, which led to secularism. According to Taylor, disenchantment "leaves us with a universe that is dull, routine, flat, driven by rules rather than thoughts, a process that culminates in bureaucracy run by specialists without spirit, hedonists without heart".[18] This is the world in which our community lives. The church must adopt a posture of active listening, of attentiveness to the disenchantment of our neighbours, in order to know how to offer something more than the deathly, heartless, hedonistic world of secularism.

3. *Collaboratively* (Partner with them): Gorringe raises various ways in which the church can collaborate with their neighbours: as the source of confession and forgiveness; as the repositories of memory and tradition; as the purveyors of justice and mercy; as the brokers of a new conversation about the future of the city. Who else is invested in meeting the needs of the community and committed to working together in a multi-disciplinary manner to meet those needs? Churches sometimes defraud their

mission of alerting others to the universal reign of God for the sake of building their own kingdom. Just like any entrepreneur, they can be overly concerned about their return on investment. But if we truly take a kingdom approach to restoring our cities, we should be willing to partner with other churches, businesses, city officials, and social organisations to meet the needs of the city.

4. *Sustainably* (Stay with them...for a long time): The people who build our neighbourhoods have no long-term interest in them. They are concerned chiefly with obtaining approvals so that they could build and sell their houses and leave town in a cloud of dust after they've closed out. Is it not possible that church planters and other professional clergy can be seen the same way? Many of them are around for long enough to close out their deal (or vision, as they like to call it) before moving on to the next venture. Perception is reality until we change it. Like a marriage, church leadership should be for the longest time, to be wedded to a community through thick and thin, come what may. As Wendell Berry points out, "Make a home. Help to make a community. Be loyal to what you have made. Put the interests of your community first. Love your neighbours — not the neighbours you pick out, but the ones you have".[19]

Mission-As-Place as a Spiritual Practice

The Missional Network, headed by Alan Roxburgh, has been encouraging an ongoing engagement with the idea of mission in a particular place as a spiritual practice. The Network began initially to answer a question posed by Lesslie Newbigin over thirty years ago: What is the nature of a missionary encounter with the late modern culture that shapes the West? Their answers have led them to the following five convictions:

1. Because the missionary God is at work in the shifting, turbulent contexts of Western societies, the churches are called to enter a new imagination for being God's people;

2. This requires disciples of Jesus to be shaped by disciplines and practices;

3. Local contexts are where God's ordinary people discern the activity of God;

4. The Spirit is leading us on a journey of mutuality and respect toward our neighbourhoods and communities;

5. There are no preferred solutions or formulas. Experimentation and innovation are important gifts for this journey.[20]

On the basis of these convictions, Roxburgh then turned his attention to the idea of mission-in-place as a spiritual practice, or more accurately, a series of practices. What rhythms of life or habits will sustain us as we seek to live in embodied, incarnational ways in the communities in which God has placed us? When one considers the usual life of the typical church it is plain to see that it has inculcated shared practices among its members — weekly attendance at worship, daily prayer, group study of the Bible, etc. Roxburgh's questions have to do with whether there are other, or even different, practices we are better off promoting. He says,

> Such a re-imagining requires the church, first and foremost, to ask what it means to be re-socialized into a way of life that posits the gospel as an alternative narrative to that of late modernity. This is a *prima facie* requirement of a missionary encounter with our culture. How do we take this journey? What are the guides for this strange path on which God's Spirit is leading us?

In answering his own question he turns to Jesus' commissioning of his disciples in Luke 10: 1–12. This is an oft-quoted text in missional church circles, and at times I fear too much can be made of it. It is neither a magic formula nor a blueprint for all Christian mission. I don't believe Jesus was establishing the *exact* shape of Christian mission for all the ages in Luke 10. Indeed, it is clear that the passage needs to be read in light of Luke 8 — the parable of the sower and the seed — where Jesus explicitly states that in this phase of the kingdom of God the message must be broadcast far and wide, and as quickly as possible. Knowing that some seed will fall along the path, some on rocky ground, some among thorns, and some still on good soil, the imperative at this stage of his ministry seems to be to scatter the message as broadly as possible. This in turn makes sense of his instructions to his disciples in Luke 10 to wipe the dust from their feet and move on should a town or village not accept their message. Of course, this is the very opposite of what we've been discussing — a long-term commitment to the same people in the same place. Jesus' is conscious of his limited time. He must disseminate his message as widely as he can, so he instructs his disciples to leave unresponsive communities, something that has been used by itinerant evangelists to justify their trans-local ministries for centuries. Let me say, I do believe some of us will be called to trans-local work, but they are the exceptions who prove the rule.

Nonetheless, I agree with Roxburgh that the greater use of Luke 10 lies in the way it has set an alternative missional posture for the followers of Jesus, one that can be readily embraced even by those of us who choose to stay put in the neighbourhoods to which he has given us. Firstly, as Roxburgh says, it "re-orients the *focus* of the church's activities from within and among themselves into the communities where they dwell".[21] This is unmistakable in Luke 10. There is no prefabricated ministry, no prepared suite of missional products to be presented, no firm model of church. The commissioning of Luke sets the followers of Jesus on a decidedly outwardly oriented trajectory. Secondly, Roxburgh says it "reframes the *location of the questions*" asked by the disciples themselves. Rather than making ecclesiocentric enquiries the disciples are forced to interrogate the situation differently. Their questions are theocentric. An ecclesiocentric question would be, "How do we fix the church?" Whereas a theocentric one is, "How do we discern what God is doing ahead of us in our communities?" This shifts the agenda from asking what *we* should do, to an exploration of how we are to join with what God is already doing ahead of us in our communities. From there Roxburgh then distils a series of practices from the text. As I mentioned earlier, these oughtn't to be seen as a straightjacket, or a fixed blueprint, but rather as a collection of habits that can be worked out differently in their unique situations.

The passage begins: "After this the Lord appointed seventy-two others and sent them two by two ahead of him to every town and place where he was about to go. He told them, 'The harvest is plentiful, but the workers are few. Ask the Lord of the harvest, therefore, to send out workers into his harvest field. Go! I am sending you out like lambs among wolves'" (Luke 10:1–3). What follows is a series of instructions, or to use Roxburgh's parlance, "a set of practices that shape their journey". They are:

- *Operate in community.* The disciples are sent out in pairs, ensuring that their missional DNA is rooted in a social construction rather than individualism. I am not suggesting that like Mormon missionaries we should duplicate this exactly and start knocking on doors in pairs. Rather, I think it is important that as we seek to re-embody our faith in context, we should be seen as serving alongside others. Join the PTA *with others*. Eat regularly in the same coffee shop *with others*.

- *Collaborate with the neighbourhood.* This point was made earlier, but I reiterate it here in light of Jesus' advice to his followers that they not take a purse or bag or sandals on their journey (v.4). At the very least this would force them to become dependent on the hospitality of their host community, ensuring a mutual collaboration or partnership in their endeavours together.

- *Declare the shalom of God.* As Alan Roxburgh points out, this was not a polite, formal greeting. These disciples were walking where the Roman empire had previously proposed their *Pax Romana*. If the residents of the towns they visited remained loyal to Rome then they would be offered a measure of security. The message of the disciples was that shalom came from only God. It was a radical counter-narrative to the imperial control of Caesar. An important spiritual practice today must be the speaking of an alternative story to the American and Australian dreams or the promises of middle-class security.

- *Identify persons of peace.* Much has been written in recent times about the importance of the discovery of "persons of peace" in a host community. Alan Hirsch and I wrote about this in *The Shaping of Things to Come* when we said, "People of peace are key people who are spiritually open, have good reputations, and have influence in the community".[22] In Luke 10 we see Jesus instructing his disciples to look for such people (v.6). That is to say, those people who accept the radical declaration that the shalom of God trumps the specious claims of the *Pax Romana* are the ones with whom the disciples are to spend their time. Paul followed this approach in Corinth by focusing his efforts in the home of Priscilla and Aquila, the local tentmakers (Acts 18:1–4). Likewise, we need to move into the neighbourhood, making radical declarations about the peace of God and look to see which influencers rise to the calling.

- *Enter into the social rhythms of your community.* Having identified such persons of peace, Jesus then says, "Stay there, eating and drinking whatever they give you, for the worker deserves his wages. Do not move around from house to house" (v.7). This has become one of the greatest challenges to the church today. And yet we are called to humbly and graciously submit ourselves to the social rhythms, diet and practices of the community, rather than forcing them to submit to ours. We delight in the stories of Hudson Taylor and other great pioneers of nineteenth-century mission to China, and the way they shaved their heads and grew pigtails and tied them in top knots. We hear of the wearing of Chinese dress and eating Chinese cuisine, practices that were considered scandalous in their time, and we consider them heroes. And yet appearing to judge our neighbours and refusing their offers of hospitality has become standard practice in many churches today.

- *Heal the sick.* Enough said? Remember, the miracles and the parables were signs that the universal reign of God had broken into the world. They were authentications that Jesus is Messiah and Lord. We too are instructed to make signs of God's reign clear today. These will include social justice, joy, beauty, peace and mercy. But they will also include the healing of the sick and the deliverance of those held captive.

- *Announce the universal reign of God.* This is the most impressive aspect of the mission of Luke 10. When the disciples are instructed to declare their message, it is this: ". . . tell them, 'The kingdom of God has come near to you'" (v.9). Having previously announced the shalom of God — his mercy and favour in setting all things to rights — the disciples must now tell those with whom they've broken bread and whose hospitality they have accepted, that the kingdom of God *is near*!! Imagine a Jewish family in Tyre, in Galilee, in coastal Joppa or in Beersheba in the south being told as they sit at their family's dinner table that the kingdom of God is near. For them, the kingdom or presence of God was only found in Jerusalem and even there only in the temple. And yet one of the spiritual practices of the earliest followers was to identify the grace and power of God in revealing his reign and universal rule to be present everywhere, always.

These ancient practices call us into place. They insist we live out our faith, not in church worship services and Bible study groups alone, but in relationship with our neighbours, in compassionate, humble, collaboration with others and focussed on the glory of the triune God. One of my great inspirations in the discussion about a re-engagement with place is the Kentucky writer and pastoralist, Wendell Berry. He has written a meditation on the importance of long-term connection to the land and the intimate relationship between the earth and human culture:

> For many years now my walks have taken me down an old fencerow in a wooded hollow on what was once my grandfather's farm. A battered galvanized bucket is hanging on a fence post near the head of the hollow, and I never go by it without stopping to look inside. For what is going on in that bucket is the most momentous thing I know, the greatest miracle that I have ever heard of: it is making earth. The old bucket has hung there through many autumns, and the leaves have fallen around it and some have fallen into it, and the fallen leaves have held the moisture and so have rotted . . . This slow work of growth and death, gravity and decay,

which is the chief work of the world, has by now produced in the bottom of the bucket several inches of black humus.

I look into that bucket with fascination because I am a farmer of sorts and an artist of sorts, and I recognize there an artistry and a farming far superior to mine, or to that of any human. It collects stories too, as they fall through time. It is irresistibly metaphorical. It is doing in a passive way what a human community must do actively and thoughtfully. A human community, too, must collect leaves and stories, and turn them to account. It must build soil, and build that memory of itself — in lore and story and song — that will be its culture. These two kinds of accumulation, of local soil and local culture, are intimately related.[23]

Chapter Two

MISSION AFTER CHRISTENDOM

STUART MURRAY WILLIAMS

In post-Christendom, the church is that community of people who look to discover what God is actively doing in the world around them and then join themselves to that work. The church is that community of people gathered around Jesus Christ in order to participate in his life and incarnate it into the context where he has placed them. — Tim Keel

The Demise of Christendom

I collect post-Christendom anecdotes — signs that the long era of Christendom in Western culture is coming to an end:

> The Somerfield supermarket chain issued a press release in March 2007 reporting how many Easter eggs would be eaten over the Easter period but noting that very few people knew how eggs were related to the birth of Jesus celebrated at Easter. A revised press release was issued two days later reporting that very few people knew how eggs were related to the re-birth of Jesus celebrated at Easter. Two days later a third press release was issued saying that very few people knew how eggs were related to the resurrection of Jesus celebrated at Easter. Got it! These press releases were drafted by an intelligent graduate working for a PR firm, who had no idea of the Christian story.

> A Baptist minister named Mary was obtaining some foreign currency from a shop in a town in England using her credit card and passport. The English woman dealing with her was suspicious because the credit card gave her name as Mary but on the passport her first name seemed to be Rev. But the Muslim woman working alongside her said: "That's okay — it just means she's a holy woman". A Muslim introducing a Christian to a post-Christendom secularist.

See, we are moving out of one mission context and into another. This emerging mission context is not necessarily tougher than the context with which we have been familiar — in fact, it may offer fresh possibilities — but it is really different and we will need to develop new ways of thinking and acting. I want to explore the strange new world of post-Christendom in this lecture and identify some of the challenges and opportunities it presents.

I have proposed a definition of post-Christendom: *Post-Christendom is the culture that emerges as the Christian faith loses coherence within a society that has been definitively shaped by the Christian story and as the institutions that have been developed to express Christian convictions decline in influence.*

Post-Christendom implies institutional and ideological transitions: the churches and other Christian organisations become increasingly marginal in size and influence; fewer people know the Christian story, understand Christian language or recognise Christian imagery; diverse religious and secular philosophies compete for influence in the space previously occupied by Christianity; and the churches need to renegotiate their relationship with the surrounding culture.

The situation is complicated by several factors, not all of which we can examine in detail here:

- The overlap between eras and paradigms as Christendom gradually unravels;

- The many vestiges of the Christendom era that will cling to church and society for many years yet;

- The variety of ways in which Christendom is disintegrating in different nations;

- The global context of continuing (and in some places explosive) church growth, within which Western societies are exceptional; and

- The use of post-Christendom terminology as a synonym for post-modernity.

Post-Christendom is a provisional term for a transitional period in Western culture. Like all "post-" words, it is backward-looking and tells us little about where we are heading. In this twilight zone, this liminal place between eras, we will need to be patient, courageous, humble, tentative and flexible.

Christendom is waning across Western culture but at different rates and in different ways — not surprisingly, given the different histories of different nations. Not all have had state churches like most European nations: the US has had constitutional separation of church and state; Germany has had a peoples' church rather than a state church. In some nations the demise of Christendom has been almost imperceptible over many decades; in others it has been dramatic and very rapid — in Montreal, for example, church leaders report church attendance dropping from 25 per cent to 4 per cent in ten years). Post-Christendom looks different in Catholic and Protestant contexts. Sometimes the secularism that results is laissez-faire; in other places it is aggressive and seeks to restrict religious influence.

Some have suggested that the US is and will remain an exception to this trend. Philip Jenkins, author of *The Next Christendom*, makes such a claim. Clearly, church attendance is still much higher than in most other Western nations, and is buoyed further by waves of immigrants from the global south. And evidence is emerging of disturbing collusion between the Bush administration and conservative evangelicals that might, if unchecked, have resulted in a new and worrying version of Christendom. But research indicates that churchgoing in America is less than half the headline figures and declining, although the readiness of many Americans who do not attend church to tell researchers that they do indicates that Christendom instincts still persist in many parts of the US.

You will know the Australian situation far better than me. In Britain the three-way and deep-rooted connection between church, state and monarchy complicates matters, but the disestablishment of the Lutheran Church in Sweden suggests that, with persistence, such links can be unravelled. Much more tenacious are the numerous vestiges of Christendom scattered across Western culture — symbols, buildings, institutions, mindsets, values and assumptions. Some may regard these as treasures to be guarded or points of connection that are still useful in mission; others want to sweep them away so that true Christianity can emerge free from the trappings and detritus of imperial Christianity.

This complex and evolving situation is further complicated by the ways in which the term "post-Christendom" is used in missiological circles — and increasingly in local churches as this way of characterising our mission context gains currency:

- Some use the term simply to acknowledge that our context has changed and we can no longer behave or operate as we used to. There is no need for disavowal of those aspects of Christendom that we now regard as utterly inconsistent with the teaching of Jesus; no need for repentance for the corruption and coercion that oppressed millions for centuries in the name of Christ; no need for discernment as to what to carry with us from the past as resources for the future and what to leave behind as baggage that will weigh us down. Post-Christendom has pragmatic and tactical implications for mission, but it invites no ethical or theological reflection.

- Others use the term interchangeably with postmodernity, not least in emerging church circles where postmodernity is the dominant conversation-partner and it is often assumed post-Christendom is another way of describing the same reality.

These uses of the term "post-Christendom" are understandable but problematic. They are understandable because "post-Christendom" and the weightier term "post-Constantinian" are rooted in the dissenting radical tradition that can be traced back at least as far as the sixteenth-century Anabaptists. Summarising a collection of concerns about the influence of the Christendom system on hermeneutics, Christology, missiology, ethics and ecclesiology, this term functions as short-hand (almost code language) for an alternative paradigm. The contemporary usage of "post-Christendom" does not usually connect with this history of dissent or engage with most of these concerns.

Conflating post-Christendom and postmodernity is problematic. There are, of course, areas of overlap and mutual reinforcement between these culture shifts, but they are not the same. Postmodernity does present new challenges and opportunities for mission, but post-Christendom places other important issues on the agenda that may be ignored if the terms are confused, and offers insights into some of the struggles emerging and inherited churches are facing.

For example, welcoming post-Christendom as a conversation-partner in the emerging church conversation might offer insights into why mission — and especially evangelism — is so deeply unpopular in many emerging churches. It might also help bring greater balance between cultural attunement and counter-cultural deviance. It might open up new ways of looking at the relationship between belonging, believing and behaving; encourage fresh ideas about discipleship and how churches can be learning communities; and stimulate further reflection on the ethical issues of violence and economics that are so crucial in contemporary culture (modern or postmodern).

So let me state my understanding of the paradigm shift represented by post-Christendom by noting seven transitions which characterise our emerging mission context:

- *From the centre to margins*: in Christendom the Christian story and the churches were central, but in post-Christendom these are marginal.

- *From majority to minority*: in Christendom Christians comprised the (often overwhelming) majority, but in post-Christendom we are a minority.

- *From settlers to sojourners*: in Christendom Christians felt at home in a culture shaped by their story, but in post-Christendom we are aliens, exiles and pilgrims in a culture where we no longer feel at home.

- *From privilege to plurality*: in Christendom Christians enjoyed many privileges, but in post-Christendom we are one community among many in a plural society.

- *From control to witness*: in Christendom churches could exert control over society, but in post-Christendom we exercise influence only through witnessing to our story and its implications.

- *From maintenance to mission*: in Christendom the emphasis was on maintaining a supposedly Christian status quo, but in post-Christendom it is on mission within a contested environment.

- *From institution to movement*: in Christendom churches operated mainly in institutional mode, but in post-Christendom we must become again a Christian movement.

Post-Christendom can easily be perceived as a threat and associated with failure and decline. Our response to the challenges it presents may be to burrow ostrich-like into the remaining sand of familiar church culture, scan the horizon for growing churches that proclaim we can continue doing what we have always done, or clutch desperately at promises of revival or programmes that promise to restore our fortunes. Indeed, the more we understand post-Christendom, the greater may be the temptation to respond in such ways: post-Christendom is not an easy environment for discipleship, mission or church.

But the perspective of this lecture is different. It celebrates the end of Christendom and the distorting influence of power, wealth and status on the Christian story. It grieves the violence, corruption, folly and arrogance of Christendom. It rejoices that all who choose to become followers of Jesus Christ today do so freely without pressure or inducements. It revels in a context where the Christian story is becoming unfamiliar and so can be rediscovered — by Christians and others. It welcomes the freedom to look afresh at many issues seen for so long only through the lens of Christendom. It anticipates new and liberating discoveries as Christians explore what it means to be a church on the margins that operates as a movement rather than an institution. And it trusts that history will turn out how God intends with or without Christians attempting to control it.

The Emerging Mission Context

What, then, will characterise mission after Christendom? How will we incarnate and declare the good news of the kingdom in this transitional period and in whatever post-Christendom becomes?

The first five of the seven transitions mentioned earlier are happening whether we like it or not. We can choose how to respond to these changes, but we cannot resist them. But the final two transitions are challenges: can we find the courage and grace to transform our churches, denominations, seminaries and organisations from institutions primarily involved in maintenance into a new missionary movement fit for the emerging culture?

Proposing a paradigm shift from "institution" to "movement" often provokes a sceptical response. Some assert the sociological inevitability of movements becoming institutions. All renewal movements throughout church history have followed this course, losing their missional impetus and adopting institutional characteristics in order to survive. Even the first-century Jesus movement became institutional! Christendom may then represent the maturing rather than subversion of the Christian movement. So why bother advocating a shift that will be temporary?

But even if this process is inevitable, we might still do well to re-imagine ourselves as a movement. Church history reveals the interplay of periods of institutionalisation and renewal movements. Some movements thrived for decades and sparked fresh initiatives. On the threshold of post-Christendom, even a temporary shift is worthwhile; remaining in institutional mode will be disastrous. Furthermore, there are organisational processes whereby movements can be revitalised rather than succumbing to institutionalisation.

Proposing a paradigm shift from "maintenance" to "mission" also invites scepticism. This shift is sometimes misrepresented through unwarranted polarisation. Mission without maintenance is clearly unsustainable. Dividing activities into static categories labelled "maintenance" and "mission" is also simplistic.

However, caricature and polarisation aside, challenging the maintenance orientation that marginalised mission during the Christendom era is vital. Mission *is* the church's agenda; maintenance comprises crucial items on that agenda. This mission shapes the church, and appropriate maintenance sustains it. Missiology precedes ecclesiology, not vice versa.

We will return shortly to consider some of the practical implications of these transitions, but first we should flag up three key contextual questions posed by post-Christendom. If we are to become a missionary movement, with what issues will we need to engage?

First, there is ongoing and vigorous debate among sociologists and missiologists about whether the demise of Christendom will eventuate in a thoroughly secular society or in a reconfiguration of religious and spiritual impulses. In the 1960s confident assertions that Western culture was becoming ever more secular and that religion would practically die out were commonplace. Some still promote this secularisation thesis in one form or other. But religion appears to be taking as long to expire as a Shakespearean actor; indeed, some suggest that rumours of its death have been exaggerated. The irritation and increasingly belligerent reactions of secularists have been very apparent in Britain in the past couple of years, as have some indications of more aggressively secular strategies, including the idea of renaming Christmas as "Winterval" and attempts to ban the wearing of religious symbols or garments at work. Secularism may be emerging as the new fundamentalism in Western culture.

Other sociologists and many missiologists present evidence — researched or anecdotal — of renewed, vibrant but disparate spirituality and new religious expressions across Western societies. They note, for example:

- Evidence from polls and surveys of widespread enthusiasm for and diffuse experiences of spirituality;

- A burgeoning market in spirituality and spiritual elements in popular culture — films, magazines, songs, games, etc.;

- Testimony from youth workers of interest among young people in various forms of spirituality; and

- The influence of New Age spirituality, paganism and Eastern religions.

Many emerging churches have bought unreservedly into this prognosis, bewailing the secularity of inherited churches and developing styles of worship and community they hope can connect with this resurgent spirituality. They are under no illusions that this spirituality is essentially Christian, but they regard spirituality as the focus for mission in postmodernity. Some inherited churches share this perception and are busy repenting of the secular values they have imbibed. Much Christian youth work and many evangelistic strategies are predicated on convictions about a rising tide of interest in spirituality and openness to the numinous.

But how prevalent is this interest in spirituality, how significant is it, and how long will it last? Steve Bruce, an unrepentant advocate of the secularisation thesis, discounts the evidence for spiritual resurgence. In the uncompromisingly entitled *God is Dead*,[1] he systematically deconstructs the case for spirituality returning to the cultural centre, debunking suggestions that the evidence amounts to more than ephemeral phenomena around the fringes of a secular culture.

Other researchers and sociologists interpret the evidence differently, especially those who believe human beings are innately and incorrigibly religious and that Western secularity is exceptional and an inadequate long-term basis for society.[2] Many Christians who agree with this hope that the resurgent interest in spirituality they detect, despite the scepticism of secularists, offers fresh opportunities for mission if we can transform our churches to engage with a more spiritual culture.

But defining the centre of our culture in terms of spirituality — and shaping our churches and mission strategies in light of this definition — may be precipitate. At least we should be asking some searching questions before putting all our eggs in this basket:

- Is the interest in spirituality mainly confined to white middle-class westerners? If so, our reshaped churches and mission strategies will reach only one section of society — the section we always seem to prioritise.

- Is the interest in spirituality only temporary? Generation X may exhibit hunger for spiritual experience, but Generation Y may be less interested.

- Is contemporary spirituality a designer accessory that does not engage people at depth or impact their core beliefs, values and priorities? If so, it may not be a stepping-stone towards Christian faith but inoculation against it.

- Is contemporary spirituality instinctively, and often explicitly, post-Christian or anti-Christian? If so, hopes that spirituality may be a conduit into Christian faith and church may be unfounded.

- Is post-Christian spirituality fulfilling the role allotted to Christianity since the Enlightenment — satisfying private spiritual needs without challenging secular values at the core of society? If so, mission in post-Christendom may require renewed engagement with secularism — perhaps as our main priority.

None of this implies post-Christendom churches should miss opportunities to urge those interested in spirituality to explore Christianity. Nor should we refrain from planting new churches configured for this context, or duck the hard challenge of reorienting inherited churches that have been more profoundly warped by secularisation than we have realised. But we will beware identifying spirituality as the centre of post-Christendom society and developing ecclesial or missional responses shaped exclusively by this aspect of culture.

Second, there is the issue of how we relate to and engage with other faith communities. Although representatives of these communities were present in the Christendom era, they were minorities in an overwhelmingly dominant "Christian" society in which the spiritual and cultural superiority of Christianity was assumed and none-too-subtle attempts were made to persuade such minorities to convert and conform to the imperial ideology. But in post-Christendom these communities are present in greater numbers, have heightened visibility through their dress, architecture and cultural expressions, enjoy protection from discrimination, and offer other religious options to disillusioned Christians and secularists.

Post-Christendom is a contested religious environment within which Christians appear as one minority among others, albeit a minority with memories of majority status struggling to adjust to this new reality. We are not used to engaging with other faith communities on a level playing field. Nor for centuries in Western societies have we acknowledged other faiths as conversation-partners in the development of theological and ethical thinking, as they were in the pre-Christendom period, and as they have been in many other parts of the world. And within our churches profound ignorance, caricature, fear and uncertainty are hindering gracious and sensitive missionary responses to this emerging context. Witness the reaction of an elderly churchgoer in Oxford recently who refused to believe a speaker in a multi-faith conversation was an English convert to Hinduism: "but he can't be — he's much too nice!"

Mission after Christendom in a multi-faith society will surely involve:

- Educating Christians about the beliefs and practices of other faith communities, presenting these fairly and rejecting stereotypes and caricatures;

- Encouraging friendship between people of different faiths and exploration of the riches of these diverse spiritual traditions;

- Exploring partnership and mutual support in the face of aggressive secularism so that the "rumour of God" is kept alive in Western culture;

- Engaging in respectful and open dialogue that recognises shared convictions and investigates important differences in belief and practice; and

- Inviting friends from other faith communities to follow Jesus and welcoming the opportunity to learn more about him ourselves through these encounters, as Peter did in the house of Cornelius.[3]

My suspicion is that this will prove to be one of the most important missiological issues in the twenty-first century. If we learn how to engage creatively, peacefully and truthfully with other faith communities, what emerges could refresh our theology, transform our divided neighbourhoods, form a bulwark against secularism, and even prevent global catastrophe. Representatives of the Muslim community dismissed the "Winterval" idea as nonsense and rejected the secularist notion that Christmas was offensive to Muslims in a plural society. People of faith may disagree passionately on some issues of belief and practice, but we may often choose to make common cause in the face of intolerant secularism. But if we retreat into narrow sectarianism, hide behind prejudice, make common cause with Western secularists rather than other people of faith, or sink into the morass of relativism, we face a bleak future in a world riven by religious extremism and policed by secularists who do not understand how most of the world thinks.

Third, there is the question "what is the gospel?" I confess to being somewhat weary of the question "what is church?" which seems to preoccupy so many Christians in inherited and emerging churches today. Although this question is necessary as we reconfigure our churches for postmodern, post-Christendom societies, sifting through inherited structures and processes, rhythms and rituals, assumptions and expectations, I fear too often we are actually falling into the Christendom trap of putting ecclesiology before missiology. We might do better to ask what the good news is in post-Christendom and shape our churches in light of what we discover. This might not only restore the precedence of missiology over ecclesiology but set both in the context of Christology as we rediscover the Jesus story and learn to tell it afresh in our generation.

In Britain for the past two or three years a highly charged debate has been preoccupying evangelicals, prompted by comments from a high-profile Baptist evangelist and social entrepreneur, Steve Chalke, who has suggested that penal substitution is an unhelpful and flawed interpretation of the atonement that does not resonate well with contemporary culture.[4] At Steve's invitation I was drawn somewhat reluctantly into this debate, which has generated considerable vitriol and has demonstrated the extent to which evangelicals seem to be locked into this particular way of explaining the significance of the death of Jesus. This is not the place to rehearse all the arguments, but two observations are relevant to this lecture:

- Many evangelicals have been encouraged by this debate to acknowledge their discomfort with explanations of the gospel that seem rooted in retributive and violent interpretations of the cross. These may have been persuasive during the Christendom era, but they are now widely perceived as problematic.

- The debate has encouraged some to look afresh at the Gospels and to explore the meaning of the death of Jesus in relation to his life and his resurrection, aspects often marginalised by the penal substitution approach. Some are asking "what is the gospel?" and are discovering fresh ways of telling the Jesus story and other ways of explaining the significance of his death, often drawing on interpretations that are much older than penal substitution and resonate with the pre-Christendom churches.

Post-Christendom, unlike Christendom, is not a "guilt culture": human beings may be as guilty as we ever were before a holy God, but such guilt is not widely felt or recognised. Many new Christians — 50 per cent in one influential study — report that they had no sense of guilt when they became Christians but were searching for God for other reasons. Many report also that their awareness of guilt grew as they joined churches, engaged in worship and became disciples, but it was not the starting-point in their Christian journey.

Searching for other starting-points as we present the gospel in post-Christendom need not be dismissed as watering down the gospel or colluding with contemporary culture. Might it not rather be drawing on the wealth of images and motifs in the New Testament, all of which are needed to explicate the extraordinary grace of God, and engaging afresh in the task of contextualisation which marks all authentic missionary engagement with culture? Christendom made normative a particular interpretation of the gospel that was originally an attempt to inculturate the gospel into a particular mission context — medieval and early modern Europe. Missionaries then exported this interpretation as normative and orthodox into other cultures as Christendom extended its hegemony. But in post-Christendom we need to revisit this and find ways of announcing good news that are fresh, contextual and faithful. We do need to ask again, in conversation with our culture and with the Christian community through the centuries, "what is the gospel?"

Becoming a Missional Movement

Post-Christendom is a demanding but invigorating mission context. As we wrestle with these and other issues, we need to return to the question we left hanging earlier. What might be involved in becoming a missional movement in post-Christendom?

This paradigm shift will require imagination and persistence in many dimensions of the Christian community. I have time here only to offer a sample of what might be involved.[5]

What might it mean in the local congregation?

- Introducing the concept of *missio Dei*. First propounded by Karl Barth in the 1930s, this post-Christendom perspective on mission is very well known among missiologists now, but almost unknown in local churches. But it is liberating and agenda-shifting to recognise that mission originates in the character and creation-wide purposes of God, not in the church; and that becoming a "missional church" does not mean embarking more enthusiastically on a set of mission activities but encountering afresh the missionary God.

- Developing a pattern of congregational prayer that embraces the broad agenda of God's mission, including the needs of the local community, the systemic violence and injustice that causes global suffering, the groaning of creation, and the call to make disciples of all nations. Infusing corporate worship with songs and prayers from the world church, with contextual liturgies that earth the church in its own community, and with testimonies celebrating signs of God at work in the world.

- Equipping Christians firstly to participate in God's mission and only secondly in church activities. Introducing regular opportunities to reflect theologically about vocational, cultural and ethical issues, ordaining church members when they start new jobs or take on new roles in the community, and encouraging them to think missionally about their work, networks and neighbourhoods.

What might it mean for denominations?

- Appointing to trans-local roles people with pioneering and strategic gifts, rather than experienced pastors reputed to have "a safe pair of hands", men and women who are mission-minded and committed to envisioning, risk-taking and change-management.

- Catalysing strategic church planting that pioneers fresh expressions of church on behalf of the denomination, offering pioneers freedom to experiment and supportive accountability. And introducing a parallel "church pruning" strategy, whereby unhealthy churches that discredit the gospel and deflect resources from mission are encouraged to close.

- Committing to spend over half of denominational funds on mission, recognising that this redistribution of resources will profoundly reshape the denomination. Merely using missional language can be comforting but deceptive. Finance is a measurable indicator of progress towards this paradigm shift.

What might it mean for training institutions? The Christendom mindset pervades many theological colleges and their influence will scupper progress unless they embrace this paradigm shift. It might mean:

- Adapting their selection processes to ensure they recruit mission-oriented students with the character and skills for ministry in post-Christendom. Disavowing their bias towards the pastors and teachers who dominated the Christendom era and welcoming the opportunity to train apostles, prophets and evangelists.

- Revising their curricula: not just adding mission modules or specialist courses but teaching *all* subjects from a missional perspective and training *all* their students for cross-cultural mission. Teaching them to interpret Scripture with a consistent missional hermeneutic.

Let me offer a few final comments in the form of questions, identifying some other issues that there is no space to develop further but that may be worth pondering further:

- How significant for a missional movement is our tone of voice? The Christendom era was characterised by churches using an imperialistic, moralistic and superior tone of voice, as seemed to befit a dominant institution. This was never appealing and is now offensive and inappropriate. Can we learn to speak more graciously and winsomely?

- How important for a missionary movement is healthy tension between incarnation and attraction? Some are vigorously promoting incarnation — embodying gospel and church in diverse contexts beyond the congregation — and seem to denigrate any attempt to attract people into the Christian community as dualistic and rooted in Christendom ecclesiology. But pre-Christendom churches were powerfully and unashamedly attractive. And Christendom represents an incarnational approach that downgrades distinctive Christian communities. In post-Christendom can we not embrace both the "salt" and "light" images in our missiology?[6]

- How vital for a missionary movement is another healthy tension between being culturally attuned and counter-cultural? Authentic contextualisation requires both dimensions — what mission historian Andrew Walls names as the "indigenising" and "pilgrim" principles.[7] Cultural attunement may be chronologically the first aspect of a truly missionary encounter with any culture, but the counter-cultural aspect cannot be indefinitely delayed. Can we build missional communities in post-Christendom without a contemporary form of catechesis to detox converts and induct them into a different way of living shaped by the story of God?

- How crucial for a missional movement is a commitment to non-violence? Not just because we live in a world that believes the myth of redemptive violence, and not just because we want to disavow the violence of the Christendom era, but because peace, *shalom*, is at the heart of the gospel and the reconciliation of all things is at the heart of *missio Dei*. Is a missional church also necessarily a peace church?

- What images shall we use to identify ourselves and to inspire hope as a missional community in post-Christendom? We need more than strategies and theology: we need imagination. Michael Frost, following Walter Brueggemann, offers "exiles" in his recent book.[8] Stanley Hauerwas adopts a pre-Christendom term rooted in the New Testament — "resident aliens (*paroikoi*)".[9] My friend and colleague Noel Moules suggests "shalom activists". I wonder what post-Christendom Australians might call themselves?

Chapter Three

FITTING INTO THE TRIUNE GOD'S MISSIONAL PLOT

MARY FISHER

The Bible is concerned with God's purpose of blessing for all the nations. It is concerned with the completion of God's purpose in the creation of the world. It is not — to put it crudely — concerned with offering a way of escape for the redeemed soul out of history, but with the action of God to bring history to its true end. — Lesslie Newbigin

A Conversation in Peking

Sometime between January 1978 and July 1987 I was seated in the Peking Hotel in the capital city of the People's Republic of China. My best friend and I were talking. He was a young Chinese writer working for the main literary magazine in China. We had been fellow students at China's Nankai University in years prior to June 1982.

Our focus of discussion — the Genesis creation narratives and the chapters up to Genesis 12. We were comparing Genesis with the creation narrative of Babylon. The Babylonian epic of creation heralds Marduk as the god of Babylon. Marduk worship shaped all that was involved in maintaining the status quo of the once dominant nation state of Babylon. Step by step we were comparing the narratives.

The Babylonian epic regards nature as divine. That may appear to us as ancient thinking. But that thinking is a reality which still exists in many parts of the world today. And the consequences are astounding. In India today cows are treated with more value than many of the Dalit human class, the class known as the "untouchables". And this in the land that is expected in the next 50 years to be the most populous nation in the world.

But how else is this divinising of nature affecting India? If you Google the topic "Monkeys invade Indian capital" you will find this report from the BBC of January 9, 2001. This is one of many reports I have seen since I first saw a news story about monkeys and Delhi around 1999.

> Thousands of monkeys are invading government buildings in Delhi, forcing employees to arm themselves with sticks and stones in case they are attacked. At least 10,000 monkeys are creating havoc in the Indian capital by barging into government offices, stealing food, threatening bureaucrats and even ripping apart valuable documents. The increasingly aggressive animals swing effortlessly between the offices of the Defence,

Finance and External Affairs Ministries and some have even been spotted in the Prime Minister's office.

"They are moving in very high security areas", says Defence Ministry officer, IK Jha.

Officials say there is little that can be done. Killing the animals is not an option because monkeys are a sacred symbol in Hinduism, India's main religion.

Last year in October the following report was written:

> The deputy mayor of the Indian capital Delhi died a day after being attacked by a horde of wild monkeys. SS Bajwa suffered serious head injuries when he fell from the first-floor terrace of his home on Saturday morning trying to fight off the monkeys. The city has long struggled to counter its plague of monkeys, which invade government complexes and temples, snatch food and scare passers-by. The High Court ordered the city to find an answer to the problem last year. One approach has been to train bands of larger, more ferocious langur monkeys to go after the smaller groups of rhesus macaques. The city has also employed monkey catchers to round them up so they can be moved to forests. But the problem has persisted.
>
> Culling is seen as unacceptable to devout Hindus, who revere the monkeys as a manifestation of the monkey god Hanuman, and often feed them bananas and peanuts.

India does not have Genesis 1 at its foundation. As a result, the deputy mayor of Delhi died less than six months ago. Foundational worldviews have implications for how we inhabit the world in which we find ourselves.

But what does that have to do with my friend and me sitting together in the Peking Hotel working through some of the main points of Genesis 1 to 11? We worked through the radical nature of Genesis 1 de-divinising the nature gods that the people surrounding Israel worshipped. Genesis 1 is clear. Nature is not divine. And as we talked about the implications of nature being seen as divine we spoke of the poverty of India — China's next door neighbour.

In Genesis 1 humans are the climax of the creation. They are the image of God — each of astounding value. Genesis 1 confronts one of the foundational reasons India is so poor. Rather than understanding nature within the context of stewarding nature for human good, India still deifies nature like Babylon did thousands of years ago. In the Babylonian epic humans are seen as beings created to be the slaves of the nature gods. India today is influenced by such a view.

And so I sat with my friend comparing the amazing ordering of Genesis 1 where humans are made the climax of the creation narrative, humans made in the image of God. And we compared it with the chaos of the Babylonian creation myth where gods war against each other and humans are made to be slaves to the nature gods.

And as we spoke of the Creator revealed in Genesis 1 we also reflected on the desire for public education in the West centuries ago by men such as the famous Bible translators Wycliffe of the fourteenth century and Tyndale of the sixteenth century. They desired that all should be able to read the Scriptures so that people might know they were made in the image of the Creator of all that there is.

We studied this ancient text, Genesis, which elevated human persons to such glory compared with polytheistic literature. We considered at length how we are made in the image of the living Creator God and what that means for all humans everywhere.

And as we talked of Genesis we further considered the sixteenth-century philosopher-scientist Francis Bacon, the father of modern scientific method. He had been moved to develop his inductive method of scientific investigation by his study of Genesis 1. Professor Herbert Butterfield of Cambridge University in *The Origins of Modern Science* says, "Bacon held that if Adam, owing to the Fall, had lost for the human race that domination over the created world which it had originally been designed to possess, still there was a subordinate command over nature, available if men worked sufficiently hard to secure it, [even] though this had been thrown away by human folly."[1]

And so centuries ago Bacon, with his worldview shaped by Genesis 1, heralded a new age for science in which nature was perceived by him as the object of human investigation for the "charity" of humankind, as Bacon calls divine love in his writings. Compare this with the fact that the deputy mayor in Delhi just last year fell victim to a worldview where nature is regarded as divine.

The people of India are subject to a worldview which permits them to be subject to nature's whims, while the Genesis 1 account says we are to have dominion — not exploitation — dominion which requires we have good stewardship of nature for the benefit of all creation, particularly human persons.

As we continued studying Genesis 1:26–28 we considered how slavery had become illegal in the Western nations through the work of men such as William Wilberforce, whose concern arose from knowledge that all races were made in the image of the living Creator God.

We spoke of Amy Carmichael who in the eighteenth and nineteenth centuries educated little girls who had been forced out of their Indian homes to serve at temples, often entering prostitution to earn money for priests. Her work developed a sanctuary for over 1,000 children, each made in the image of God.

With the example of each person building a life shaped by Genesis 1 to 3, my friend was grasping how understanding the beginning of the story made for such a different perception of the world around us. These people of whom we spoke — Wycliffe, Tyndale, Bacon, Wilberforce, and Amy Carmichael — all had challenged the status quo of the society around them. They were "people acting up" because they understood the profound nature of Genesis 1–11.

And so as my friend and I continued to talk, we spoke of some of the other differences between the Babylonian creation narrative and Genesis 1. In the Babylonian creation narrative — as in most creation narratives I have read from many, many cultures — before the earth was ever created the polytheistic gods fought, killed each other, were jealous of each other, killed their divine offspring and the divine parents. And so, polytheistic religion is focused on the power of one of these very fallen human-like gods who gains dominance over other fallen human-like gods or over a particular area of human life. And in these polytheistic creation narratives evil is present in the creation narrative before creation is formed.

So religion grounded in polytheistic creation narratives becomes that which maintains the already unjust status quo of the particular society; serving the religious elite who worship the so-called powerful god central to state or tribal religion.

Let me repeat that: religion not grounded in Genesis 1–3 becomes that which maintains the already unjust status quo of the particular society; serving the religious elite who worship the supposedly powerful god central to that religion.

So the monkeys rule in Delhi while women whose husbands have died still are treated as less than human, even if from the highest Hindu caste — the Brahmin caste. Twice in the last twelve months I have watched programmes detailing their plight.

And in the Peking Hotel my friend and I spoke of the radical difference of faith grounded in Genesis 1–3. Here is not found a religion which seeks to maintain the status quo of any particular society. No. Genesis 1–3 is a clarion call not to be the maintainers of the status quo of any nation state; for all societies the other side of Genesis 3 are fallen societies. And the holy, loving Lord of Creation in setting forth his story calls those following after him not to be maintainers of the status quo where it does not reflect the character of the triune creator and covenant God known through divine acts in history. Why?

The status quo in every society manifests, at some point, our rebellion against God. The creator God, the covenant God of Israel, the triune God revealed in the first-century trinitarian Jesus of Nazareth event, calls us *not* to accept the status quo. Rather we are called to be salt and light in any society in which we find ourselves.

And so my friend and I continued discussing the triune God's Israel story. We spoke of the gift of the law of the Creator and how a woman, Huldah, a prophetess, had called people in the Old Testament back to submission to Yahweh. That a woman surrounded by men in the text was given such a role is in itself a challenge to the patriarchal society of ancient Israel as found in 2 Kings 22.

And the Creator's character of holy love manifest through his Ten Words or Commandments to Israel at Mount Sinai, and the voice of the prophets throughout Israel's history, all call us not to maintain the status quo of fallen societies — rather our calling is to be salt and light.

And we spoke of people throughout history who, in understanding the story of the Christian Scriptures, have pushed back the consequences of the Fall by being salt and light. We spoke of many people who had been salt and light throughout history, and my friend began to weep and weep and weep. We were being stared at. The Peking Hotel was at the time the major hotel in Peking. But this brilliant young man wept and wept, regardless of all who started watching.

You see, in talking about the radical nature of Genesis 1–3 compared with other creation narratives, my friend had come to understand that the God of all Creation was calling all humanity to understand that the world as it now exists is not as the Creator would have it to be.

Human persons have not sought the fellowship of the Creator. In fact, in Genesis 2, humanity has preferenced the word of the creature over the Word of the Creator, and have continued to do so to this day.

And even when the Word that Eve and Adam reject in Genesis 3 becomes flesh and dwells among the Israelites under first-century Roman oppression, again those who claimed to follow the creator covenant God of Israel did not receive that Word. And so John says in John 1:10–11, "He was in the world, and the world came into being through him; yet the world did not know him. He came to what was his own and his own people did not accept him".

And my friend understood why, in all our discussion of Christianity, I had mentioned how often we who should be salt and light have been hijacked by the culture, by the nations of which we are a part.

We spoke of the terrible revolutions of so-called Christian Europe during the eighteenth and nineteenth centuries which attempted to overcome cruel rule but led to new tyrannies; and how the British Isles had escaped the bloodshed because of the preaching of Whitfield and the Wesley brothers. And my friend wept. He had come to understand how the people of God being salt and light could impact whole societies.

In theological terms, he came to understand that the church of Jesus Christ, the eschatological community indwelt by the Spirit of God, is called to be the witness of the in-breaking of the kingdom of God in the trinitarian first century Jesus of Nazareth event.

In a world marked in every aspect of life by the consequences of human rejection of God, we are called in our witness to Jesus Christ to push back the Fall as we submit ourselves to be shaped by the only truly revolutionary religious narrative there is. In calling us to be salt and light, the triune God's missional plot of Scripture does not permit us to be people who maintain the status quo. As salt and light, we are "people acting up". And so Wycliffe and Tyndale, shaped by the triune God's missional plot in so many ways, were regarded with loathing by parts of the ecclesiastical hierarchy. Wycliffe's body was dug up by church authorities and his remains caste out from his sacred burial site. Tyndale was strangled by the executioner and then his body burnt at the stake. Wilberforce faced two decades of opposition before finally seeing his anti-slavery laws pass through parliament. Amy Carmichael was an affront to much of the religious system around her in India.

As salt and light, not submitting to the fallen status quo of any society is not the culturally acceptable path to take. In fitting into the triune God's missional plot, such people are regarded by those maintaining the fallen status quo as people acting up, people threatening societal harmony.

But we are called into a narrative where the Creator God desires to dwell with human persons; a narrative where, in Genesis 3, human persons prefer the word of the creature over the Word of the Creator and have continued in this way; a narrative where we are invited to participate in the Creator's pursuit of humanity; a narrative where, following the creator covenant God of a former slave people, we are called not to maintain a fallen status quo; a narrative where we are called to be salt and light; a narrative where we are called to be people acting up, not accepting the status quo of fallen reality.

But the revolution against a fallen status quo into which the triune Lord of Creation calls us is not a revolution of angry power seeking It is a revolution of servant love wherein we are called to image the Creator of all that there is in creating space for others. We are called to fit into a narrative where we are to create shalom space for the benefit of others; so that those who do not know the creator covenant God might know something of the holy love of the Father, the Son and the Holy Spirit.

My friend was beginning to understand that the triune God's missional plot was not only about personal conversion; it was about human persons inhabiting the world in such a way that dehumanising status quos were challenged; inhabiting the world in such a way that injustice was not accepted; inhabiting the world in such a way that repentance was to be manifest both personally *and* societally.

It was about participating in what the triune Lord of Creation is about in calling us to more than just life as a forgiven people. It was about imaging the creator covenant God of Israel who, since Genesis 1, has been in the business of creating space in which human persons could dwell — space where shalom was manifest. And the biblical concept of shalom is all about creating space where human persons can live, inhabiting and surrounded by the holy love of the triune Lord of Creation.

And so my friend wept, for he previously knew only of a privatised Christianity which only emphasised salvation after death for those who followed Jesus. He was aware that many Christian brothers and sisters saw issues of justice as political issues, not the concern of the church. He was only just starting to grasp the biblical emphasis present since the call of Abram; an emphasis on a people called into being by the creator covenant God of Israel for the sake of the whole world. The radical nature of the blessing that the people of God would be through the calling of Abram was starting to sink in.

A Conversation in Cambridge

Some 15 years later, around 1998, I was sitting in Cambridge, England with a younger brother in Christ. Today, he is a senior advisor to one of the main leaders on the international political scene. While he is not an American, we had met in the USA in 1993. Every few years he would come to where I was living to pray and talk about the powerful Israel-for-the-World story, climaxing in the trinitarian unveiling in the very Jewish and trinitarian Jesus of Nazareth event. We would talk of how and where we are to fit into what God is about, as told to us through the trinitarian Israel-for-the-World story in what we call the Old and New Testaments.

We were talking about how Christianity, sadly, often has become a religion that maintains the status quo found in different societies. We started talking about Genesis and the radical nature of the biblical creation stories when compared with all other creation stories. We spoke of how the Genesis 1 revelation tells of a place that was formless and void — *"tohuwebohu"* in the Hebrew. A space that is totally unsuitable for dwelling is made habitable as the narrative continues. God creates space for humanity to dwell in.

And the God of all creation in Genesis 2 is pictured in great intimacy in the garden space he gives to the human beings. The transcendent Creator of Genesis 1 is in Genesis 2 now called by the personal name he gave Moses. The author's intent is obvious — this is the transcendent Creator of Genesis 1 now in intimate communion with the human creature he created.

We spoke for hour upon hour of Genesis 1—11. We spoke of the essential difference between the worldview arising from pagan religions, that maintains the status quo of societies, and the worldview of Christianity where people following Jesus are called to be radical, to be salt and light.

We spoke of a triune Lord of Creation who, in the Word becoming flesh and dwelling among human beings, has invited all who would follow him to enter into what the triune Lord of Creation is doing.

And the place where we focus on how the triune Lord of Creation wants us to enter into what the Creator is doing is at a table, a table where we remember his death. A table which Luke records in the narrative of Luke 22:14–22. And having recorded the narrative of what we call the Last Supper, the very next event that happens is that the disciples argue "as to which one of them was to be regarded as the greatest".

Echoing the spirit of the pagan creation narratives, the disciples desire to inhabit a narrative that will ensure their position, their status; a narrative where their status quo is maintained. And as I look at the history of the church since the disciples, so often we have reflected the narrative of the disciples arguing over status and position, seeking to know who is the greatest; and failing to make space where those who do not know the Creator of all the world can dwell with us. Rather than acting up against a fallen status quo of society by being salt and light, we so often participate in that status quo — being no different from our neighbours.

My friend later told me that it was this conversation which had cemented in his mind that he was to try to bring kingdom values to bear on the political system of his nation; values which never maintain the status quo of fallen societies; that always call the people who would follow after Jesus to be salt and light by seeking not only personal conversion, but by challenging inhumane situations in society.

And he understands the call that was given to a slave people led by Moses. Removed from slavery, the Israelites were formed as a new people. We find this recorded with profound theological poetry in Exodus 15. It climaxes in verse 18 with the announcement that Yahweh will reign forever and ever. And then the newly formed people of Yahweh, formed as a people before they ever get to the promised land, are challenged in Exodus 19:1–6

> [1]In the third month after the Israelites left Egypt — on the very day — they came to the Desert of Sinai. [2]After they set out from Rephidim, they entered the Desert of Sinai, and Israel camped there in the desert in front of the mountain. [3]Then Moses went up to God, and the LORD called to him from the mountain and said, "This is what you are to say to the house of Jacob and what you are to tell the people of Israel: [4]'You yourselves have seen what I did to Egypt, and how I carried you on eagles' wings and brought you to myself. [5]Now if you obey me fully and keep my covenant, then out of all nations you will be my treasured possession. Although the whole earth is mine, [6]you will be for me a kingdom of priests and a holy nation.' These are the words you are to speak to the Israelites."

As the international biblical scholar and Australian native William Dumbrell points out, the word translated "although" in the phrase "although the whole earth is mine" is better translated "because". So verse 5 b and c would be better read: "Because the whole earth is mine, you will be for me a kingdom of priests and a holy nation". And Peter, in his letters, tells Christians that that is now our role, a whole people who live their lives as holy priests serving the world because the whole earth belongs to God. We are not to reflect the values of the culture around us but we are to create space in which the world can know the radical welcome of the God who, in the conception, life, death, resurrection and ascension of Jesus, so clearly provides the way for humanity to dwell with him.

But as we know, Israel and all humanity do not want to dwell with Yahweh in the space he has given them, in the way Yahweh wants them to dwell with him. And so we read that tragic narrative of Israel demanding of the prophet Samuel a king to rule over them. They already have a king, as Exodus 15:18 tells us, but as the parable of the Wicked Tenants tells us in Mark 12, Israel does not desire to dwell with the Son of the King who is sent. And that tragic parable is an echo of 1 Samuel 8:7 where God says to Samuel, "Listen to the voice of the people in all that they say to you; for they have not rejected you, but have rejected me from being king over them". So my friend and I discussed how often, even in the Christian world, we do not want to live in accord with God's gracious, holy, life-giving rule. The seven churches in the Book of Revelation witness to that reality. And they stand no more.

My friend from Cambridge daily brings his understanding of the in-breaking of the kingdom in the birth, life, death, resurrection and ascension of Jesus, and outpouring of the Spirit by the Father and the exalted Lord Jesus, into the decisions his nation is making.

In a world where power seeking is constant, he seeks to ensure that the narrative of the missional plot of the triune God of history shapes what he raises as most important. He is seeking to be salt and light.

A Conversation in Soweto

Over the years, I have spent many hours speaking with different people about how we as the people of God are to be inhabiting the world — fitting into the plot of the triune God's missional narrative. One of the most profoundly challenging persons I ever have met is Caesar Molebatsi, a pastor in Soweto South Africa. Caesar was well known long before apartheid disappeared. He was mistrusted by the Afrikaan authorities because he was a black pastor in the township of Soweto. Black radicals did not like him because he was not supportive of the manner in which they sought change. The world of evangelical Christians was suspicious of him because he was an important person in the famous black township of Soweto where trouble for the apartheid government was a constant reality. He lost a leg through the driving of a drunken white man, but there was no anger in him toward this man.

As he spoke to me of his ministry, the narratives to the church found in Mark 8 came to mind. Jesus takes his disciples to Caesarea Philippi — a place of great degradation. Rabbis writing after the time of Jesus announced that when the Messiah they were still expecting came — they had rejected Jesus as Messiah — Caesarea Philippi surely would be destroyed because of its great degradation. Central to that city's degradation was the worship of Pan, carried out on a site which still can be seen today. There worshippers participated with priests and priestesses in sexual relationships.

When Jesus brings his disciples to this place where he first is acknowledged as the Christ, the anointed King of Israel, by Peter, Jesus mentions not a word about the chaotic lifestyle that is centred there. In acknowledging Peter's recognition of him as the Christ, Jesus does not focus on the sinfulness of those at Caesarea Philippi. Rather he speaks of his own death and calls those who would follow him to journey in the same way.

It is not from a stance of denouncing the sin of the surrounding society that Jesus manifests his calling as Messiah. Rather, while journeying to the cross, it is by sharing fellowship with prostitutes and sinners that he makes known the amazing love of the Father as manifest in the story known as the Parable of the Prodigal Son. And he calls those who would follow him to journey in the same way.

Caesar Molebatsi did not accept the status quo of the white oppressive regime; nor did he accept the status quo violence of the black revolutionaries. Rather, seeking to manifest the way of the cross in ministering to all, he found himself suspect even to those who would call themselves evangelical brothers and sisters in Christ. As we talked, I found it so ironic that he who had followed Jesus had been given the name of Caesar, the name taken by emperors in a family who declared themselves to be lord of the universe, hope of the world.

Caesar Molebatsi was salt and light by *not* maintaining the status quo of apartheid South Africa; he was salt and light by *not* maintaining the status quo of radical black revolutionaries; he was salt and light by *not* maintaining the status quo of the evangelical church who did not know what to do with this man who maintained no status quo set by fallen humanity.

And so he understood the narrative that calls us into the missional plot of the triune Lord of Creation who, in Jesus, does not become the reviler of sinners but rather creates space in which he dines with them. Caesar Molebatsi, in the face of profound suspicion from each of those communities, continually created space for any who would come. Perhaps more than anyone I know, he perseveres to this day in the way of the cross — following Jesus.

A Conversation in Sydney

Then last year I was sharing here in Sydney with a group of people about the story of Scripture, the Israel-for-the-World story climaxing in the creator, covenant God of Israel being unveiled as Father, Son and Holy Spirit in the trinitarian Jesus of Nazareth event. We were discussing how God is a Creator who constantly uses space to manifest the divine desire to dwell with people — people whom he desires to free from slavery to sin. We spoke of Genesis 1, the whole world as the Creator's gift to us as a place in which we can dwell. We spoke of Genesis 2, that amazing narrative of great intimacy where the Creator is in the garden with his creatures. We spoke of being removed from the garden and what that represents; we spoke of the flood story manifesting — as William Dumbrell's scholarship points out — that sin brings about uncreation. The flood story is a reversal of the language of Genesis 1. We spoke of people being led out of slavery in one country into a different space. We spoke of the people with whom Jesus constantly hung out, the people for whom he created space. We spoke of the cleansing of the temple as an indictment of worship there. We spoke of Paul's language in Romans 5–8, where he echoes Exodus language as he explains the new space the triune Lord of Creation has led us into. In and through Jesus and through the Spirit, God has freed us from the slavery of sin. And with each narrative we were discussing, the astounding manner in which the creator God uses space to manifest his love for human beings was evident.

Perhaps for us today the story of the cleansing of the temple is one of the most prophetic challenges for understanding how we are to fit into what God is doing in the world and how the triune God's missional plot reflects how God is creating space for others to dwell with him.

Jesus comes into the temple after arriving in Jerusalem, told in Mark 11. He has just been claimed as King by Israelites who lay down palm leaves, the symbol of the revolution that had occurred almost 200 years earlier by Jews led by the Maccabean family who were revolting against Antiochus Epihanes.

In Mark 11:11, Jesus goes into the temple and, according to the Scripture, "looks around at everything". In the following verses we see him leaving the temple and the next day Jesus curses the fig tree, then he re-enters the temple and overturns the money tables in the Court of the Gentiles, and then again attention is drawn to the now-withered fig tree.

In announcing the judgment on the temple as he overturns the money tables and in not allowing anyone to carry anything through the temple he says, "Is it not written: 'My house will be called a house of prayer for all nations'? But you have made it 'a den of robbers.'"

Three things are happening here. The first quote is from Isaiah 56 — a short chapter of twelve verses. Isaiah 56:1 says, "Maintain justice, and do what is right". From verse 3 onwards Isaiah starts speaking of the foreigner, those not of the line of the covenant people, and the eunuch — he who is not sexually whole. Jesus quotes from verse 7 of Isaiah 56.

> . . . these I will bring to my holy mountain
> and give them joy in my house of prayer.
> Their burnt offerings and sacrifices
> will be accepted on my altar;
> for my house will be called
> a house of prayer for all nations.

And verse 8

> The Sovereign LORD declares —
> he who gathers the exiles of Israel:
> "I will gather still others to them
> besides those already gathered."

Jesus is announcing judgment on Israel's worship where the worshippers are using the Court of the Gentiles to enable their own worship. The very manner in which Israel, God's covenant people, were focusing their relationship with Yahweh on setting up their own worship was such that those whom God would bring into his worshipping community were excluded. Those who were not of his covenant line, the Gentiles, and those who were not sexually whole, in this case the eunuchs, were not welcome in the temple. Jesus continues from Jeremiah 7:11, "but you have made it a den of thieves".

This is a word that starts in Israel's God saying to Jeremiah:

> ²Stand at the gate of the LORD's house and there proclaim this message: "Hear the word of the LORD, all you people of Judah who come through these gates to worship the LORD. ³This is what the Lord Almighty, the God of Israel, says: 'Reform your ways and your actions, and I will let you live in this place. ⁴Do not trust in deceptive words and say, "This is the temple of the LORD, the temple of the LORD, the temple of the LORD!" ⁵If you really change your ways and your actions and deal with each other justly, ⁶if you do not oppress the alien, the fatherless or the widow and do not shed innocent blood

in this place, and if you do not follow other gods to your own harm, ⁷then I will let you live in this place, in the land I gave to your forefathers forever and ever. ⁸But look, you are trusting in deceptive words that are worthless. ⁹Will you steal and murder, commit adultery and perjury, burn incense to Baal and follow other gods you have not known, ¹⁰and then come and stand before me in this house, which bears my Name, and say, We are safe — safe to do all these detestable things? ¹¹Has this house, which bears my Name, become a den of robbers to you? But I have been watching!' declares the LORD."

What is happening here? Israel was meant to be a kingdom of priests and a holy nation for the sake of the world which belongs to the God of Israel. But, in not being who they were supposed to be, they were robbing the rest of the world of the heritage of knowing the God of all creation. And as Jeremiah continues his profound judgment comes to a climax with these words:

²¹This is what the LORD Almighty, the God of Israel, says: "Go ahead, add your burnt offerings to your other sacrifices and eat the meat yourselves! ²²For when I brought your forefathers out of Egypt and spoke to them, I did not just give them commands about burnt offerings and sacrifices, ²³but I gave them this command: Obey me, and I will be your God and you will be my people. Walk in all the ways I command you, that it may go well with you." ²⁴But they did not listen or pay attention; instead, they followed the stubborn inclinations of their evil hearts. They went backward and not forward.

So the worship of Israel is being judged for Israel's not being who their creator, covenant God has called them to be.

When Jesus uses the words "you have made it a den of robbers" the New Testament account uses a Greek word for "robbers" which is not simply a household thief. The phrase here "a house of robbers" has particular emphasis in the time of Jesus. The word "ληστων" a plural possessive term qualifying the temple as a house that belonged to the *"leisteis"* was astounding. Why? For the ληστης or *"leisteis"* were those who were zealots opposing the Roman rulers. They robbed the wealthy and used the money for their revolutionary purposes.

Jesus is declaring that by the very manner in which Israel was worshipping, the foreigners who were occupying the land were being excluded from worship of Yahweh by the people worshipping in the temple. They were stopping the Romans from the possibility of coming into the court of the Gentiles. Instead of being a people who opened the possibility for the foreigner who is their oppressor to come to know Yahweh, they wanted them out.

It is to a people oppressed by the most cruel Roman empire that Jesus says, "Love your enemies". Read the Sermon on the Mount in terms of it being to an oppressed people who wanted the Romans out of Israel, and you begin to understand in a small way the cost of servanthood that Jesus is calling them to.

A Roman centurion, at the time of Jesus' death, stands at the foot of a cross on which is written in three languages the title "King of the Jews". It is this man, whose job was oppressing the covenant people of the creator, covenant God of Israel, who first announces "Truly this man was God's Son". God is the Creator who, ever since Genesis 3, has been seeking to bring those who would be the enemies of God into relationship with the creator covenant God of Israel for the sake of the world. So the sign of the slavery of Yahweh's covenant people Israel to first-century imperial Rome becomes the symbol that the kingdom of God is here — but is not like we so often want it to be. The kingdom embraces those the covenant people regard as their enemies. The implications of that for us today are most profound.

Space, as God uses it, is ultimately for the sake of those who do not yet know of the holy love of the triune creator, covenant God. The thrust of the plot of Scripture since Genesis 1 always has been that the creator God calls a people to himself for the sake of those who do not know who the creator of all the world is.

The fig tree being cursed before the temple judgment by Jesus, and withering afterward, is not simply an interesting little comment about Jesus' hunger and agricultural seasons.

It is a parable about the temple. Verse 13 and 14 are stunning.

> When he came to it he found nothing but leaves, for it was not the season for figs. He said to it, "May no one ever eat fruit from you again."

Jesus is announcing judgment on Israel's temple worship. As Isaiah and Jeremiah have shown, it has not produced the fruit of Israel being the people they are called to be for the sake of the world. And the triune God of creation is revealing who God is, as the Son of God is sent by the Father in the power of the Spirit. And as this man Jesus, the incarnate Son of the Father, empowered by the Spirit, institutes the in-breaking of the rule of the triune Lord of history into human history, he calls to himself a people who, by their lives, are to be witnesses to Jesus, to his rule, and to his in-breaking kingdom. And the triune Lord expects fruit in our lives — for Jesus is now ascended to the Father and the Spirit has been poured out.

Jesus' last challenge to his disciples was a challenge to live for the sake of the world that does not know who Jesus is. As we understand where we are in the missional plot of the triune Lord of Creation, we must understand that the central plot of the biblical canon always has been missional. Even the structuring of Genesis points in that direction. Abram and Sarah are called by the Creator to begin the narrative plot that will solve the tragic situation of all nations as depicted in Genesis 1—11.

Moses is called to lead a people who are called to be a kingdom of Priests and a holy nation because the whole world is Yahweh's. Israel, in rejecting Yahweh as their king, seeks a human king. Yahweh will use this rejection to show what true human rule should look like in the person of the incarnate second person of the Trinity, sent of the Father, empowered by the Spirit. His is a rule manifested by holy love, a love that is prepared to die for the sake of those who would follow him.

But Yahweh cannot allow his covenant people Israel to live in the illusion that they can continue in the space he has given them while not living in accordance with their creator, covenant God's word — and exile results.

But even then, as shown in places like Jeremiah 29, the creator, covenant God of Israel is seeking the shalom welfare of those who would be at enmity with him.

> Also, seek the peace and prosperity of the city to which I have carried you into exile. Pray to the LORD for it, because if it prospers, you too will prosper.

However, the covenant people of God yearn to return to their land. Even after they return they are ruled by foreign kings with their gods. They believe themselves still in exile while inhabiting their land; Yahweh, and his anointed, are not to be seen as king. But they believe they will again be released from slavery, that Yahweh will return to Zion, as Isaiah proclaims, and that evil will be defeated.

Jesus of Nazareth arrives on the scene as Israel yearns for return from exile with the establishment of their own anointed king. They yearn for forgiveness of sins as exile and foreign domination are all focused by the prophets on punishment for sin. They yearn for the return of Yahweh to Zion, for nowhere after Ezekiel 8—12 do we hear of the glory of the Lord returning to the Second Temple. They yearn for defeat of evil, which the Essenes see as all those not part of their community, and the Pharisees see as the Romans and the many who are not obeying the law. Debate continues as to how Yahweh will again rule his kingdom with Herod, the Sadducees, the Pharisees, the Essenes, and the John-the-Baptist group each having their own perspective.

Into this debate comes a man, Jesus of Nazareth, who is announcing — the kingdom of God is here but it is not like you thought it would be, Israel. And through his birth, life, death, resurrection and ascension and, with the Father, pouring out of the Spirit at Pentecost, Jesus redefines what the rule of the triune Lord of Creation is all about. And his rule is always always always missional.

Most of us have been raised in church institutions, whether Catholic or Protestant, which focus the whole communal life of the church toward the event we call "worship service".

But the call of Jesus to us must be focused through a call to mission, for he says that as the Father sent him in the power of the Spirit he, the exalted Lord Jesus Christ, now, in the power of the Spirit, sends us.

There are no options. We, the people of God, are called to be a missional people. And if we really understand the verbal nature of mission, the active nature of mission, we will understand it is never an activity that maintains the status quo of any society we find ourselves in. Like Caesar Molebatsi, our lives will be so different that all around will find us different; in some cases the difference will be a threat.

By not being maintainers of the status quo, we will be marked by being a blessing to others who are not followers of Jesus of Nazareth. Like Abraham, our lives will bless others; like Moses, we will understand that our calling is for the sake of all of God's world; like Jeremiah, we will seek the welfare of our enemies; unlike most of Israel's kings, we will not seek our own welfare but will follow the way of the cross of Jesus. And always, we will be seeking to create space for those who are not yet followers of Jesus Christ.

What does that mean for the people who claim to follow after Jesus Christ? It means everything is to be understood through the lens of mission, of being salt and light, of making the holy love of God known to a world that has no idea of the love of God.

The triune Lord of Creation has called us to participate with him in creating space for others through a remembering that calls us to the Table of the triune Lord of Creation. In coming to that table, we come to a table that only comes into being because of the love of God the Father. In coming to the table to fellowship, we come to a table that celebrates the way of the cross as central to the life Jesus invites us to participate in. In coming to the table, we come knowing that the Spirit of the living God calls us away from that table to serve a world that does not yet know the triune Lord of Creation — who once again is seeking to draw them into a space where they can dwell with the creator.

The church is confronted with a choice. We can participate in the triune God's missional plot: becoming a people, not fitting the status quo, living our lives for others, seeking the welfare of the alien, the stranger, hanging out with those who would never dream of entering a building our society calls a "church"; ultimately being witnesses to who Jesus is; becoming a people who many would regard as "acting up".

Or we can continue in a way that is leading to increasing isolation of people who claim to follow Jesus from the society around them that perceives them as judgmental.

At a foundational level every local church body must ask itself whether what it is doing is creating space for the person who does not know Jesus to experience the loving grace of the triune Lord of Creation. Our following Jesus is always to be a calling wherein we remember that, as the Father sent the Son in the power of the Spirit for the sake of the world, Jesus sends us in the power of the Spirit as his people for the sake of the world. Becoming a people who don't maintain the status quo is not optional.

Now why do I tell you these stories? I speak of these stories because for many years I, like so many people, had no idea how the biblical canon fitted together as one story: a story where the creator, covenant God of Israel wants to form a people who, like him, will create space for people to dwell with the Creator of all that there is — Father, Lord Jesus and Holy Spirit.

As a journalist covering a story, I came to know Christ through a community who were making space for the drug addicts and street kids of Brisbane. I did not believe a word they told me, but in their life as a community I saw ordinary people making space for what I regarded as the dregs of society. They did not accept the status quo of the city of Brisbane, but challenged it by lives lived for the sake of people I regarded as the dregs of society. They were creating space for others.

In China for almost a decade, I saw a society where the status quo of the ruling communist elite was maintained at the cost of anyone who got in the way. And the story of disciples from Mark 8—10 was constantly before me. Remember, Jesus says he has to go to Jerusalem and die, and calls them to a similar path. And the disciples reject this way of serving the God of Israel, arguing about who is the greatest among themselves.

In China I came to realise that all humanity seeks to maintain its own self-interest, the status quo that best serves what they want. Humanity fails to love. But the triune creator, covenant God has called us into the divine missional plot. If we participate, we will be seen by many people as acting up.

But then that is why Jerusalem and Rome hung Jesus on a cross — he didn't fit either the religious or political status quo — he was acting up. And the Father, through the Spirit, vindicated him. He was raised that we might follow in Jesus' ways.

Chapter Four

FOLLOWING JESUS INTO SUBURBIA

SIMON CAREY HOLT

Make a home. Help to make a community. Be loyal to what you have made. Put the interests of your community first. Love your neighbours — not the neighbours you pick out, but the ones you have. — Wendell Berry

Introduction

On a visit to the National Gallery of Victoria in 2007, I joined the throng of Melburnians cued to see a retrospective exhibition of the Australian artist Howard Arkley. Arkley is commonly celebrated as the foremost painter of Australian suburbia. His abstract images are a celebration of ordinary suburban homes and their interiors. Throughout his career, Arkley was fascinated with the vernacular and domestic spaces of daily life. His studio was not in a trendy inner-urban laneway but in Melbourne's south-eastern suburb of Oakleigh, the centre of what historian Graeme Davison calls the 1960s "cream-brick frontier" of Melbourne.[1] Arkley's view of the world was an unashamedly suburban one. Though I had seen his images before, viewing them firsthand and within the hallowed walls of the NGV was disconcerting. The three-bedroom brick veneer of my childhood hung alongside renowned works by Renoir and Picasso. Here art and life collided and, to be honest, it felt odd.

At first glance, the idea of following Jesus into suburbia is similarly awkward. Discipleship in suburbia? Surely not! Isn't real cross-bearing discipleship about the courage and cost of self-denial? Suburbia, that familiar middle-class cacoon of self-interest, is surely the epitome of all we are called to leave behind; a spiritual cul-de-sac of familiar and well-feathered nests that dulls us to the radical call of Jesus; a residential island of affluence and uniformity that numbs the soul, repels difference and prioritises personal comfort and security. Doesn't the call to *go* demand that we relinquish such lukewarm incubators in favour of the furnace of real and exotic mission elsewhere?

Awkward indeed, yet Arkley's images remind us there is more to suburbia than meets the eye. The awkwardness arises out of assumptions that rest on old and tired binaries. The caricatured perspectives of the suburbs these binaries produce know very little of the complex world the suburbs of today have become and offer little help to those of us seriously engaged with the nature and practice of Christian mission in Australia.

The truth is, we inhabit the most suburban nation on earth. Despite our dominantly rural mythologies of verandahs, rocking chairs and gumtrees, over 75 per cent of Australians reside in the suburbs, those sprawling habitats of detached, single-family homes on individual blocks of land that fan out in every direction from our urban centres. There's barely a verandah in sight.

Residentially, we are now a nation of suburbs with urban and rural fringes.[2] As Australian economist Tony Dingle has noted, the outer suburbs of our cities have always been the nation's main "breeding zone".[3] For the majority of Australians, life begins, unfolds and ends in the suburbs. It is my view that missional practice in Australia — practice that is genuinely contextual — has no choice but to take suburbia seriously, something I suggest we have not done with any intentionality or creativity to this point.

In the United States, a small trickle of books has appeared calling Christians to a more intentional engagement with their suburban context. In the best of these, *The Suburban Christian*, Albert Hsu provides a reasoned but passionate plea for a deeper and more strategic investment:

> God needs suburban Christians who are willing to take a sharp look at their environment, recognize the challenges of the suburban setting, and then stay here to do something about it. Some Christians live in suburbia because it is a fulfillment of their personal . . . dreams for comfort and prosperity. Others are here only out of necessity and would gladly move away at the drop of a hat. Some love it here, some hate it. Many are indifferent. But whatever we may feel, for whatever reason we came, as long as we are here, the call is the same: Seek the welfare of the suburb while living in it.[4]

In our county, one described as "more relentlessly suburban"[5] than any other, this is a plea worth sharing. The suburbs are more than just a place to lay our heads; they are the containers of our lives, formative containers which shape us in ways we barely appreciate. Whatever our motivation for being there, the suburban context deserves a more thorough exegesis than we have yet had the inclination to provide.

With this in mind, this paper will proceed in three parts. Firstly, I will explore the forces — cultural, theological and missiological — that have rendered suburbia the forgotten land. Second, I will consider factors of contemporary suburban life that make it a land of opportunity in the mission of the church. And thirdly, drawing upon J B Jackson's metaphor of the home as a hand, I will suggest the beginnings of a methodology for mission in suburban Australia.

I. Suburbia: A Land Forgotten?

A. Culturally Marginalised

In a 1960s issue of the literary journal *Meanjin*, the noted journalist Allan Ashbolt provided a characteristic critique of Australian suburbia, one that epitomises the "anti-suburban orthodoxy" that held sway in intellectual circles for the last half of the twentieth century. According to Ashbolt, the 1960s suburbanite was a kind of humorous and debased caricature of the Australian pioneer:

> Behold the man — the Australian man of today — on Sunday morning in the suburbs, when the high-decibel drone of the motor mower is calling the faithful to worship. A block of land, a brick veneer, and the motor mower beside him in the wilderness — what more does he want to sustain him, except a few beers with the boys, marital sex on Saturday nights, a few furtive adulteries, an occasional gamble on the horses or the lottery, the tribal rituals of football, the flickering shadows in the lounge-room of cops and robbers, goodies and baddies, guys and dolls.[6]

According to Ashbolt, the life of the suburban resident was but a poor reflection of the real thing. This caricature was a critique of the margins from the perspective of the centre. Provided by the so-called "central city elites", it cast the city as a place of diversity, difference, creativity, culture, energy, ideas and radical politics. By contrast, suburbia is a bland monoculture of dull monotony, mimicry, social order, apathy, conformity and conservatism.

More than fifty years later, this old orthodoxy has been challenged,[7] yet something about it continues to limit, even haunt, the Australian imagination. In a commentary on the recent artistic responses to suburbia, the journalist James Button suggests that the old orthodoxy is alive and well.[8] He quotes the *Age* film critic Adrian Martin who believes that Australian films like *Travelling Light* and *Muriel's Wedding* have "created a cliché of orderly, miserable streets, houses laden with kitsch, and overwrought mothers with hair in rollers". Why, Button wonders, are so many film makers and artists driven by a such a "fierce, upwardly mobile desire to attack or escape their own daggy origins?" Why are the suburbs never seen as "places where real people live real dramas and real lives?" Indeed, the word "suburban" has become part of common vocabulary to describe the mediocre, ordinary and run-of-the-mill.

There has been much written this past decade about the rise of the McMansions, those oversized, cookie-cutter homes constructed at breathtaking rates on the fringes of our cities. Indeed, these homes and their estates are an easy target for those with a point to make about suburbia, and the commentary illustrates the continuing chasm that exists between the centre and periphery. The *Sydney Morning Herald's* architecture critic Elizabeth Farrelly famously described one such estate, Kellyville in Sydney's north, as "heartbreakingly, wrist slittingly ugly . . . a land of obesity . . . (that) leadens the soul."[9] Understandably, the residents of Kellyville were incensed. One wrote a letter to the editor, telling Farrelly:

> My wife and I know perfectly well how to brief an architect, but at the moment we'd rather put our resources elsewhere. In the end we must do what is best for our

kids, and that's where Kellyville shines . . . Sneer through the steaming haze of your decaf soyaccino if you wish, but homogeneity brings a certain comfort, security and a sense of true community that other Sydneysiders can only dream about. Dare to be similar![10]

In reality, today's suburbs defy easy categorisation, either by their critics or those who defend them. The signs of class, identity and political perspective that once set them apart have given way to a much more complex, fine-grained and diffuse social and cultural geography. One only has to contrast the suburbs of Footscray and Kew, or Bankstown and St Ives. As the Australian National University's Alastair Greig has said, we can no longer treat suburban culture simplistically as though suburbia is where people think with a single mindset or speak with one voice. He calls for the old binaries of city and suburb to be put to rest in favour of a more intelligent and nuanced reading of our residential life. Regardless, the marginalisation continues.

B. Theologically Estranged

Perhaps as a consequence of suburbia's cultural marginalisation, or concurrent with it, theology and suburbia have had what might be called an estranged relationship. This estrangement is a consequence of both geography and metaphor.

(i) Geography

The Australian Jesuit Andrew Hamilton is one of the few theologians to explore the relationship between theology and the suburbs.[11] Hamilton argues that the theology's relationship to the suburbs has been modeled on its earlier relationship to the countryside — a spatial movement from the centre to the periphery: "from the cathedral, the university, the seminary, the places where theology belongs, to places where uninitiated people live."[12]

According to Hamilton, this theology of centre and periphery is one of both condescension and fear. Its condescension rests on the assumption that the natives of suburbia are uneducated, exposed to more popular forms of religious culture and practice, and in need of salvation. Its fear is found in the distance between the centre and periphery and plays both ways. Viewed from the centre, the supply lines out to these far-flung peripheries are long, both geographically and culturally. Its inhabitants may well be theologically depraved and unreceptive to the truth the theologian brings. From the perspective of the periphery, the centre is invisible, a world entirely removed from the daily routines and struggles of real life. Commonly, those at the periphery view these "ivory tower" theologians with suspicion; for they speak in a strange tongue and of fearful things that may well destroy faith rather than nurture it.

Granted, because of changes to the relationship between the city centre and the suburbs, it can no longer be said that theology is geographically constrained. Institutions of theological education are now just as likely to be suburban in location as they are urban. Still, the gulf between Parkville and Rowville, between Newtown and Campbelltown is wide, and the consequences of more traditional geography play out.

(ii) Metaphor

In contrast with and in reaction to the above anomaly of a theology packaged in one place and transplanted insensitively to another, theologians have sought more geographically and culturally sensitive theologies, theologies allowed to develop and flourish in particular contexts and challenges. Contextual theology in Australia has taken great strides in recent decades as theologians have worked toward a more vernacular theology, one that speaks out of and into the Australian context.

Useful to this process are local metaphors or images that help us to imagine theology in a more contextual way. In so doing, we have reached for images of the desert, the outback, verandahs and vast open spaces, and often to good effect. Predictably, though, these metaphors are rural. They reflect what we have for so long imagined as the heartland of our Australian identity. Talk of spiritual pilgrimage and Australians will describe the desert centre of our land or perhaps its rugged coastal edges, but never its suburban heartland. Perhaps this is because, while Australians have embraced this heartland physically, they have denied it emotionally, and with considerable success. Consequently, we have yet to imagine a theology that places our suburban identity at its heart.

C. Missiologically Ignored

In his excellent book, *Sidewalks in the Kingdom,* Eric Jacobsen grieves theology's failure to interact with the concrete realities of urban form:

> It's not that we have no interest in the city. There are numerous Christian books on the city and about urban ministry. It's just that as Christians, we have tended to treat the city as a problem to be solved or a burden to be borne. The city is largely seen as an abstract place where humanity is gathered in the greatest concentration and therefore where the problems and needs of humans are most obvious and pressing. We have not, as our secular contemporaries are beginning to do, taken seriously the physical form or context of existing cities as a viable model for shared community life.[13]

Jacobsen goes on to note the increasing number of secular authors who view the physical forms of the city, both urban and suburban, as potentially sacramental — nurturers of community, joy, beauty and connection with the past. In contrast, Christian writers on mission in Australia seem unable to interact with the physical form of these contexts, staying out of conversations on urban planning and development. According to Jacobsen, mission thinking has viewed the city as *"a place of deep human need or sometimes a place of divine possibility, but never a place with sidewalks or plazas".*[14] I would add to this that missiology has all but ignored the suburbs, even as a context of need or divine possibility. The suburb is commonly viewed as some sort of abstract extension of the city, but not a place worthy of particular recognition.

Furthermore, if suburbs are addressed, they are viewed either as a kind of purgatory — a place somewhere between the idyllic rural and the sin-soaked urban, neither here nor there — or as a place of spiritual apathy and compromise, the place for those who do not have the courage to go where the call of Jesus leads.

Though written in the North American context, several books published in the last two years illustrate the pessimistic view of suburban life that we share. David Goetz's *Death by Suburb: How to Keep the Suburbs from Killing Your Soul* begins with the premise that suburbia is a "muddy river" that cannot be stopped, a force that bloats the soul and renders one potentially dead to the presence of God.[15] Goetz suggests Christian practices to counter the "toxins" that fester in the suburban soul. Similarly, Mike Erre's *The Jesus of Suburbia: Have We Tamed the Son of God to Fit Our Lifestyle?* bemoans "the suburban Jesus" as a "tame, whitewashed, milquetoast Jesus" interested only in soothing the soul and providing a life of prosperity, comfort and security.[16] According to Erre, it is in the suburbs that we are most prone to missing the "dangerous and wild Jesus of Nazareth who beckons us beyond the safety of our small lives".[17]

When the suburbs are viewed in either way, it is little wonder that missiology has looked elsewhere.

II. Suburbia: A Land Of Opportunity

The pursuit of a sensitive and effective Christian presence in Australia can no longer live with the marginalising, estranging or ignoring of suburbia. If we are genuinely concerned for the mission of God in our context, we must surely begin by owning the overwhelmingly suburban form of our environment and identifying the legitimate human longings that underlay our suburban infatuation. If we cannot begin with an affirmation of what is good and genuinely human in suburban life, then our criticism will be skewed and ultimately unhelpful.

Critics of suburbia abound. Books with titles like *Sprawl Kills* and *Bourgeois Nightmare* leave you with the distinct impression that suburbia is bereft of anything humanly affirming.[18] However, suburbia remains the residential context of choice for the majority of Australians. Why? Not simply because they lack alternatives, but because it continues to be the best embodiment of values prized by the average Australian. It is for this reason that a growing number of cultural commentators have identified suburbia as one of Australia's great achievements.[19]

In my view, suburbia is a spiritual place, not an a-spiritual container of life, but a spiritual landscape, an urban form that acts upon the human soul. Suburbia is a place of hopes, needs and longings. It both contains those longings and shapes them. It is a central part of the suburban resident's "spiritual geography".[20] It may well be an environment that calls to the human spirit or squelches it; either way, it is a significant shaper of the soul. As such, for those committed to the mission of God, suburbia is a land of significant opportunity.

A. An Aspirational Land: Longing for Contentment

For a substantial part of its history, suburban development in Australia has been aspirational in character. From the early part of the twentieth century when the wealthier classes were fleeing the polluted and overcrowded city centres for the fresh air and space of the outlying rural edges, the lower classes have looked on with a suburban lust in their eyes. Suburbia has long provided an accessible embodiment of what the average Australian desires — a house to call home, a place of identity and belonging, financial independence, and personal security and freedom.

In our more recent history, the word "aspirational" has been used to describe the expectations of the middle majority of Australians voters, "Howard's battlers" they used to be called; those who actively seek movement in a socially desirable direction. If you are not moving progressively up the social ladder, no matter how slowly — if your lot is not an improvement on that of your parents — then something is wrong with the system.

We must surely begin by affirming that to aspire is to be human. We all aspire to be something, have something or achieve something. To aspire is to envision, to exercise faith. Without it nothing would be achieved and nothing would change. In and of itself, aspiration is a good thing. Yet there is something about the intensity of the suburban environment that can turn aspiration into a materialist obsession. At its worst, it clouds our vision and skews our sense of what is worth aspiring to.

In a recent study, the Harvard sociologist Ezro Luttmer explored the relationship between personal wellbeing and relative financial position in one's neighbourhood.[21] In other words, he was interested to understand the connection between one's personal sense of wellbeing and how the Joneses next door are doing. What Luttmer found was that an increase in my neighbour's level of income has the same negative impact on my sense of wellbeing as does the equivalent drop in my own income. Keeping up with the Joneses has never been a more pressing obsession.

In the midst of all this aspiration, contentment becomes that ever elusive goal, for no matter what we have, we aspire to bigger, better and more. Yet genuine contentment remains the longing at the heart of the suburban soul. And the gift of a lasting contentment lies at the heart of the gospel. For in Christ we are promised an end to human striving, craving and longing, a genuine and deep rest for the human soul, not just in some elusive future reality, but today.

B. A Private Land: Longing for Security

As far back as the 1930s, the great urban historian Lewis Mumford described suburbia as "a collective attempt to live a private life".[22] No doubt, privacy has long been a dominant suburban value. It is built around the demarcation of private space — yours and mine — with clearly defined neutral territory in between.

In a recent lament for the demise of the suburban lawn in Melbourne's newest estates, the writer Michael Winkler notes the role the front yard has traditionally played in marking suburban territory.

> The distance between suburban houses echoes Australians' craving for personal space. If good fences create good neighbours, large lawns provide a domestic demilitarized zone, a space of mown neutrality. I might wander onto your lawn uninvited for a chat, where I would never take the same liberty of entering your house.[23]

The need for privacy and personal territory is a legitimate one, a natural part of being human. To be human is to be at home, to experience a sense of security and belonging in a particular place. Seeking a place to call our own and guarding its boundaries once we've found it are natural instincts. Surely this need lies somewhere at the heart of the Great Australian Dream. And suburbia's unique form provides it in good measure.

I have argued elsewhere that what was once the collective pursuit of privacy has morphed into an obsessively individual one.[24] Metaphorically, the fences have gotten higher. When the pursuit of privacy becomes a completely individual endeavour, the result is not security but residential islands of fear and isolation.

In a global walking survey presented to an international conference on liveable communities in 2006, it was found that 85 per cent of Australians identify fear as the primary factor that keeps them from walking in their cities and suburbs of residence.[25] This compares to a global average of 65 per cent. Responding to these results, urban planning expert and former secretary of the Pedestrian Council of Australia, Ian Napier, said:

> I think it's endemic in our society that we are less trusting of our fellow human beings . . . the more we drive our kids to school, the more we live privatised lives, the less we are in contact with other human beings and the less we trust other people.[26]

This was certainly the finding of a major study undertaken in Berwick, an up-market suburb on the south-eastern edge of Melbourne, once a quiet rural hamlet of horse studs and dairy farms and now enveloped in the suburban spread of the city.[27]

In this study, while noting their motivation for relocating to the area as the pursuit of a safe place to raise a family, residents commonly identified the home as a fortress and expressed concern for their children's safety. The guarding of personal boundaries was a more pressing concern than actively nurturing relationship. The suburban scholar Lyn Richards says of her research in the outer suburbs of Melbourne, "The most stunning aspect of my findings was that even the most lonely people saw neighbors as a threat. Neighbors were seen as intruding on privacy, lowering land values — in short a problem."[28]

In reality, the higher the walls and more secluded household life, the more insecure we become in the world that lies beyond. In recent decades, the US has seen the extraordinary rise of the gated community. Today some 11 million Americans live in fully secured neighbourhoods complete with boom gates and armed guards.[29] Though only about 100,000 Australians live in such communities, the rapid development of master-planned estates, gated and ungated, complete with privately owned roads, recreation complexes, parks and swimming pools, has been significant.[30] What is interesting to sociologists about such communities is that the more secure and self-contained the neighbourhood, the more insecure the resident feels about anywhere else.

C. A "Utopian" Land: Longing for Community

In *The Past and Present of the Australian Suburb*, historian Graeme Davison highlights four ideologies prevalent at the beginning of the twentieth century and which together nurtured a fertile environment for suburbia's stunning growth:

(i) *Evangelicalism:* A popular Christian movement that emphasised separation from the "worldly". It encouraged the nurturing of the home and the nuclear family as the centre of religious experience and as a realm set apart from the corrupting influences of the city.

(ii) *Romanticism:* An ideology that aligned the good life with nature and the rural virtues of tranquillity and beauty. The true romantic was one in search of refuge and peace away from the chaos and clamour of the city.

(iii) *Sanitarianism:* A movement that proclaimed the deathly consequences of pollution and urban density. It embraced the suburb as the healthy, natural alternative.

(iv) *Capitalism:* Central to the development of suburbia was the individual drive for home ownership — a significant move toward full participation in the capitalist dream and a clear statement of financial status and independence.[31]

Combined, these forces remind us that suburbia's development has long been inspired by an almost utopian vision of life: a community of like-minded citizens escaping one place to reside together in tranquillity and peace in another; an imagined ideal place where the inhabitants can live the good and righteous life without inhibition or hindrance. One only has to view the advertising billboards which line the highways of our outer suburbs to see "the heady mix of dream weaving and dream believing"[32] that frames the sale of "home" in suburbia. The words "community", "security", "a place to call home" are plastered over idyllic images of children riding bikes in glorious freedom, fathers rolling in the grass with their children, airbrushed sunsets over outdoor candlelit dinners, and neighbours gathered together on decks that overlook lakes and golf courses. Of course, the reality is very different. Typically, both parents in a household will work full-time to service the mortgage, and long commutes mean one parent arrives home each night after dark to children already asleep.

In reality, families have little enough spare time to even greet the people next door let alone spend leisurely time with them.

Utopia is quite literally "not a place" or "no place". Further, it rests on the assumption that the place we currently inhabit is inadequate and less than the imagined ideal. As Eugene Peterson observes, our utopian longings blind us to the fact that "we can only live our lives in actual places, not imagined or fantasized or artificially fashioned".[33] Of course, not long after moving the fantasy crumples under the weight of the real domestic routine.

For the prospective residents of new suburbia, community remains high on the list of values. The marketers have done their homework. Community is a longing basic to our humanity — we long to belong. But the sort of community promised on roadside billboards is indeed utopian; a "no place". Fittingly, the Anglican theologian Andrew Hake calls community "an aerosol word", one that gives "a sweet scent and a hint of mist", but has little connection to reality.[34] In contrast, the reality of Christian fellowship is found in an experience of community that is real, daily and tangible, as much a reality now as one yet to be.

III. Suburbia: Metaphor & Mission

In his celebrated book *Sense of Place, Sense of Time*, the late and respected social geographer John Brinkerhoff Jackson describes the suburban home as a hand:

> It is the hand we raise to indicate our presence; it is the hand that protects and holds what is its own; the home or hand creates its own small world; it is the visible expression of our identity and our intentions. It is the hand which reaches out to establish and confirm relationship. Without it we are never complete social beings.[35]

I like this metaphor. As is the purpose of a good metaphor, it's an image that helps me to grasp something that is otherwise difficult to get a handle on. According to Jackson, the home is the hand that we raise to indicate our presence in the neighbourhood; it's an expression of our identity as a household, family, or church community. Second, the home is the hand that enfolds and protects; it's a place of refuge, healing and connection. And third, it is the hand that reaches out to initiate and confirm relationship with those around; it's an inclusive place of invitation, hospitality and welcome. For me, each of these provides a way of thinking about what it means to follow Jesus into suburbia.

1. The Hand that We Raise

The recent and devastating fires that ravaged parts of my home state of Victoria were such a graphic reminder of the role the home plays in our lives. During the weeks that followed the devastation of Black Saturday, night after night we watched on our televisions the stories of those who suffered terrible loss. We wept with those who stood awkwardly before the television cameras, their decimated homes and properties still smoking behind them. Repeatedly, we heard these brave people dismiss the loss of their homes and their possessions as nothing compared to the sacredness of life. "At least we're still here, that's what matters," they said. Of course, they were right and profoundly so. Yet as they turned away from the cameras to look back at what was gone, their tears and bewilderment betrayed the fact that it did matter, and deeply so. Places count. Bricks and mortar they may be, but our homes are us. They hold our memories, and embody our identity. They give us a sense of who we are in the world. It is for this reason that homelessness is so violating, because homes and places do matter. Where there is no home there is no belonging.

In my view, the common Christian declaration that "this world is not my home, I am just passing through" is unhelpful to mission in suburbia. To be deeply invested in our context requires that we are fully at home; that we are able to raise our hand and say this is where I belong; I am fully invested in this place and fully present. Mission in suburbia is not a well-intentioned "sortie" into a foreign land. It is about an incarnational presence. Those engaged with the mission of God in suburbia must begin by naming their own suburban identity. We are not people of another land come with the good news of a God who resides elsewhere. Rather, we are neighbours, fellow suburbanites who have discovered and continue seeking the presence and liberating power of the gospel where we are. We, too, have been drawn to suburbia by longings common to those up and down our streets. We are no different. We do not inhabit an alternative universe. Suburbia is our home.

In the Christian tradition, images of spirituality are most often tied to acts of withdrawal and relinquishment, treating all present attachments as counter to discipleship. At its core, it's a spirituality of detachment. I would argue that spirituality in suburbia requires not detachment but ever deeper attachments. In his book *The Good Life: Genuine Christianity for the Middle Class,* theologian David Matzko McCarthy calls us to just such a spirituality, one of deep attachment to the places we inhabit, treating a house and neighbourhood not as an investment in some elusive future — a commodity to be bought and sold for financial gain — but a place in which we put down our roots and invest our lives.[36] In essence, McCarthy calls for "a kind of middle-class asceticism", a simplicity and moderation of life that nurtures long-term attachments and deep, genuine investments in the people, places and things of our suburban lives. This is a counter-cultural act, a radical statement of contentment in a consumerist society that thrives on our discontent. Indeed, there is nothing more countercultural in consumer-driven suburban Australia than to say with conviction, "what I have and where I am is enough".

On an individual level, this requires that Christians living in suburbia dig deeply into the present, caring for and nurturing good neighbourhoods. According to McCarthy, "we ought to undertake small acts of living well, of preserving and caring for a place as part of our calling to friendship and peace".[37] He continues:

> With God's grace, we have the capacity to make and cultivate things and places that are truly good. In making and tending to things in this world, we cultivate human life.[38]

For the church, this intentional investment in the "now" of the church's presence will perhaps require less aspiration to becoming the large, regional congregation that draws people from a swag of suburban postcodes in favour of a deeper contentment with being a genuinely local community of faith, one that is committed to its immediate locality.

2. *The Hand that Enfolds*

We have already acknowledged the longing for security, personal territory and a place to call home is a legitimately human one. The old saying "good fences make good neighbours" is not as anti-Christian as it might sound. I have heard proponents of alternative suburban communities call for a tearing down of fences and a radical sharing of property and possessions, setting up a commune of sorts in the midst of suburbia. While I am not adverse to such calls, and in fact would agree in part, we need to proceed with an acknowledgement that boundaries are not an evil; the longing for space and personal security is God given. The desire to provide a secure space for one's family, a place in which those within feel loved, safe and welcome is a good and righteous one.

The home is the hand that enfolds those within, providing a place of refuge and genuine community. This is so both in the suburban home and the suburban church. Effective mission in suburbia requires functional, healthy households and communities of faith. There must always be a place for closing the doors and nurturing those within. The question is, what values do we engender in those who gather there?

The suburban home that many people aspire to is a fully self-contained world, proudly independent and able to meet every need of its inhabitants without reference to any outside source. Backyard swimming pools and entertainment areas with six-burner barbecues, home theatres and wireless internet access throughout, fully stocked pantries and tool sheds, and comprehensive security systems make the suburban home a fully functional fortress that has no need of anything or anyone beyond.

Similarly, the suburban church can aspire to something of the same. Ever larger facilities complete with education centres, sporting facilities, cafes and bookshops, the suburban church can become a world unto itself, a world that provides a dizzying array of programs and services which keeps it members eternally busy staffing and resourcing the church's schedule.

In the suburban context, Christian households and communities have an opportunity to embody, not a security in isolation, but a security in community. Addressing the nature of the church's mission in the city, the Archbishop of Canterbury Rowan Williams notes the problems that can arise if the local church is seen as just one interest group among many . . .

> . . . bidding competitively for scarce resources or seeking to control the self-definition of communities. The contribution of the Church must always be something on another level from that of the various bodies struggling for dominance and access. It must simply offer a radically different imaginative landscape, in which people

can discover possibilities of change — and perhaps of "conversion" in the most important sense, a "turning around" of values and priorities that grows from trust in God.[39]

In essence, we want our households and church communities to be hands that enfold those within, nurturing values that run counter to those dominant in suburbia. As we provide that "radically different imaginative landscape" that values interdependence and the security of genuine community, cooperation and connection, so our homes become places that engender hope and an alternative way of living.

If, as St Francis de Sales said, "spiritual direction begins when people are helped to walk more slowly, talk more slowly and eat more slowly",[40] then Christian households and communities have a unique opportunity to embody a genuine spiritual presence that models real security, one that issues out of community. Perhaps the focus of the suburban church needs to be less on the generation of multiple programs and services and more on enfolding and empowering its members. Churches need to be communities that enable and release the people of God to be good and present neighbours rather than workers eternally busy in the programs of the church.

3. *The Hand that Extends*

According to Jackson, the home must be more than a hand that we raise in identity and one that enfolds those within. It must also be a hand that we extend in relationship to those around us. It is a home in neighbourhood.

Environmental psychologists have long agreed that essential to the human experience of home and community is the reciprocal relationship between one's "home" and one's "horizon of reach".[41] What this means is that for the home to be a fully human place it must be one that celebrates both its internal relationships and its connection to the world beyond its front fence. Where this relationship between the internal and external is lacking, they say, the house can never truly be a home and may indeed become a fortress.

In her fascinating book *Renovation Nation,* Fiona Allon of the University of Western Sydney describes the longstanding national obsession with home ownership.[42] This obsession, she argues, is now surpassed by our infatuation with home renovations. To a degree unmatched anywhere else in the world, we are preoccupied with improving and changing what we have — upgrading, extending and modernising.

Allon cites a 2006 report which surveyed 2000 homeowners across Australia.[43] The report found that 90 per cent of homeowners are currently renovating their homes or have specific plans to do so. On average we have up to five renovation projects on the go at any one time. The two most common motivations for home renovations are increasing resale value, and enhancing our quality of life. And it seems we are prepared to spend significant amounts to make it happen. Just under 70 per cent of home renovators are spending in excess of $60,000.

While Allon has no religious barrow to push, she expresses concern with what drives this infatuation. Perhaps, she suggests, in the face of fear, terror and uncertainty, we are retreating ever deeper into our homes, obsessively feathering our own nests, cacooning ourselves from the threats of diversity and difference that push in on every side. Ultimately, Allon says, "renovations engage our imaginations but narrow our horizons, it excites our vision but limits what we see".[44] She continues:

> Rather than just restoration and renovation — defensiveness, a nostalgic embrace of previous eras, and a drawing of boundaries around what's mine and what's ours — what we need is a new culture of openness, a new ethics of connection, and a new understanding of home and our neighbours.[45]

According to Allon, there has been no more crucial time for the extending of the hand in suburbia, for what she calls that "new ethics of connection"[46] but one so beautifully summarised in the ancient biblical command, "you shall love your neighbour as yourself".

Though people come in search of utopia, that elusive experience of community, what they more commonly find is something less grand and more isolated. What Christians living and worshipping in suburbia have to offer is not utopia, a community of "no place", but a genuine and daily experience of connection in the real and ordinary places of everyday life. Loving one's neighbour is not primarily about intimacy or deep friendship. Rather it has to do with treating the neighbour as a person created in the image of God. In the face of increasing isolation, we are called back to the time-honoured practices and disciplines of hospitality in community. These practices might be as simple as the following:

- setting an extra place at the dining room table and inviting others in on a regular basis;

- sitting on the front porch or in the front yard to drink coffee instead of hiding away at the rear of the house;

- borrowing a cup of sugar from the neighbour instead of running to the corner shop;

- sharing a lawn mower or gardening tools with the neighbours;

- turning the garage or carport into a neighbourhood play space or an afterschool homework club;

- choosing to shop locally rather than driving off to the regional supermarket;

- frequenting the local park and being open to conversation and relationship.

Extending the hand in the neighbourhood is not rocket science. It's quite simple. It's not about adding complex programs of mission to the church schedule, but empowering those in the church community to open their eyes and see the opportunities for mission that already exist in the daily and mundane routines of their lives.

Renovations are a wonderful thing. My home church, located in the inner suburb of St Kilda, a place of extraordinary diversity and challenge, has recently undergone a long-overdue renovation of its small property. A community with a long history of innovative mission to the most marginalised residents, we struggled for many years with the need to do something to the decaying but endearingly daggy building we called home. Our shared aversion to the gentrification that was happening all around us made our decision-making complex and painful. Still, it has happened now and recently we celebrated the opening of our new space.

At that opening event, we were able to name the danger we had long struggled with of being sidetracked by the desire for a nicer place to call home and of losing our passion for following Jesus into the world. Jackson's metaphor of the hand reminds us that the sacredness of a building — a home or church — is an active characteristic not a passive one. It must always be the hand that we extend to those beyond in invitation and welcome. Settling down into our comfortable seats and enjoying the new colour scheme does not a sacred building make. Its sacredness is found in the living, in the going, and in the wide open door. Albert Hsu says it well:

> Whatever kind of suburb we live in and however we might construe our notion of the ideal suburban life, a more thoroughly Christian approach to suburbia will consider how the civic good can be advanced in light of the coming of the kingdom of God. For Christians, living in suburbia must be more than a private quest for the promised land or the good life. It also includes positive objectives like accessible, affordable housing for those without, and it embraces a larger vision for God's transformative work to be done in the community in relational, practical and spiritual ways. As suburban Christians we can pray, "Thy kingdom come — to suburbia! Thy will be done — in suburbia!" We can envision a community where God's good shalom is experienced by residents and visitors alike. We can begin in the suburb where we reside, and pray for God's mustard seed of kingdom influence to take root and grow.[47]

CONCLUSION

I began by describing the paintings of Howard Arkley, those abstract images of suburbia and their ability to challenge the way we look at what is otherwise such a banal aspect of life. I hope that I have at least encouraged you to take a closer look at the piece of suburbia you inhabit and in which you struggle to follow Jesus. Indeed, it may be a place of motor mowers, mortgages and the most ordinary routines of daily life, yet without doubt it is a place of God's presence and a context in which the good news of Jesus is desperately needed.

In preparing to write the book *God Next Door: Spirituality and Mission in the Neighbourhood*, I had the privilege of sitting in the homes of more than sixty households in Brisbane, Sydney and Melbourne — single people, couples and families of all shapes and sizes who professed an active Christian faith. What I heard were some of the most extraordinary stories of people living and connecting in neighbourhoods just like yours and mine. What was tragic was how few of these people were able to name their presence in the neighbourhood as missionally significant. Mission was most commonly understood as something that happened elsewhere or a program sanctioned and organised by the church.

Effective mission in suburbia begins with an affirmation of suburbia as a place of God's presence, as much a place of God's call and as rich with the possibilities of discipleship as any other place on earth. And it proceeds with the local church opening its eyes to the challenges of its immediate neighbourhood, re-embracing its identity as a truly local community of faith, and empowering and releasing its people to go into their suburbs and neighbourhoods together, embodying the values of deep contentment, real security and genuine community that characterise the kingdom of God.

Chapter Five

LOST IN SALVATION

MICHAEL DUNCAN

There is but one Church in which men find salvation, just as outside the ark of Noah it was not possible for anyone to be saved. — *Thomas Aquinas*

I am no scholar or academic, rather perhaps a pedestrian minor-prophetic thinker. The pedestrian in me stomps and walks around the place bumping into all sorts of people on the pavements of life. Without referring to their real names, I can think of Sally, for example, who claims she is a Christian but recently confessed to me, with tears in her eyes, that she became so drunk one evening that she ended up having sex with her uncle. Steve has been attending church for years and is a chronic substance abuser. His Christian friends put it down to "backsliding" but I'm not so sure?! Vicky is seriously physically disabled (or differently-abled) and from the confines of her wheelchair devotes ten hours a day to internet porn. She too attends church and prays to God.

Be it in the pews or on the pavements, I meet this kind of "christian" a lot and the minor-prophet in me is profoundly disturbed. It has been said that while a priest represents people to God, a prophet represents God to the people. A priest would gather up Sally, Steve and Vicky and take them into the forgiving, cleansing and empowering presence of an affectionate God. We prickly prophets, however, are a different breed. As "seers", we are called to see into their situation and ask "Why do they behave as they do?" and "What is God saying to them?" This lecture will attempt to answer these questions.

Rather than giving away too much about where I'm coming from and where I'm going at this point, I'll simply inform you that I'm employing an inductive approach in my argument. You may at times wonder where I am heading but, rest assured, we will get to a destination that will stimulate debate and possibly even cause some division of opinion. After all, isn't that what we prophets are supposed to do?!

I will leave the "three key points with a subset of ten" approach to the didactic educators in our midst and unapologetically employ narrative, because I have come to share a story.

By way of introduction, let me explain something of my own story. Since 1976, when I came out of the hippie drug counterculture and became a follower of Jesus, I made it my work to encourage others not only to join Jesus' merry band but to walk as he walked. I have been looking for an emerging band of believers who will act contrary to the accepted notions of the day by outrageously loving the very people whom others seem to avoid or dislike.

For 30-something years I sought to catalyse Christians into this reckless love. When one approach failed or yielded little fruit, I changed tack, always hopeful that each new way would mobilise more to the cause. As a young pastor I earnestly preached about love, believing that educational and instructive sermons would stir and transform the pew-sitters into those who would run towards people. The success rate was around 5 per cent. Desperate to reach the other 95 per cent, I reinvented myself and relocated to the slums of Manila, believing that a clarion call from the frontlines would stir the hearts of Christians.

After ten years of living in such a crucible of harsh circumstance, responses remained few and far between. Upon returning "down under", I pastored churches in Australia and New Zealand where I tried to embody Christ's teaching of "love thy neighbour". However, I soon discovered that church cultures can be intensely / stubbornly / resolutely . . . insular / isolated / withdrawn / insensitive. I thought that leading by example might work, but these congregations were more interested in keeping the church to themselves than getting alongside neighbours and strangers. This was their club and they would not easily be moved.

A decade later I gave myself to full-time itinerant preaching, going wherever I was invited, forthrightly reminding Christians to heed the command of Jesus to love their neighbour and prophetically reminding them that there will be a final Judgment based on their works.[1] I saw more fruit or evidence from this than the previous approaches, but still the majority of Christians seemed reluctant to get involved in this kind of pro-active Christian lifestyle.

Five years ago, still despairing about the unresponsive majority, I wondered if it had to do with a lack of skill-sets and confidence levels. If I explained *how* to approach strangers, then perhaps Christians would "get it" and do it. So I set up *Alongsiders Trust* and began conducting seminars throughout New Zealand, Australia and London in the hope that know-how would result in "do now". Once again, only around five per cent were responsive while the majority went back to sitting in front of the TV.

By 2007, I was in deep despair. I knew that "loving your neighbour" was difficult. As a sociology graduate I understood the factors that can inhibit people from making the effort to walk towards others. Now I was lamenting that the sociology of Christians seemed even more determinative than their spirituality. In other words, Christians were no different from others in terms of their inattention to strangers and those in need. Surely, I heard myself arguing —to no one in particular — Christians are meant to be different. If they are not, then what has gone wrong? It was at that point that I began to engage in the ecclesiological war, looking to place blame on the way that a church "does church" as the causal factor behind this indifference.

Ecclesiological Warfare

Ecclesiology has to do with the form and structure of the church and the theology that informs that structure.[2] Initially it seemed to me that there were two sides in this ecclesiological war. On one side were the *mega-churches* with their *macro* ideas; and on the other side, *house churches* and the emerging communities of faith.

Both camps have their respective stars, publishing houses, scholars and conferences. The debate between them is rigorous. Of course, both are trying to influence the majority, which is best defined as middle-sized, mainstream, traditional churches. The macro side believes that the way ahead lies with bigger churches.

Murray Robertson, Pastor Emeritus of Spreydon Baptist in New Zealand writes:

> I recently spent some time meditating on my own denomination's annual set of statistics. Being a Mainlander (South Islander), I studied the South Island. About half the Baptist churches are small churches with fewer than 100 people attending their services. But only 17% of the total number of worshippers goes to one of them. By contrast there are only seven churches with more than three hundred worshipping at them, but these seven account for 44% of attenders... Interestingly, of those who attend a Baptist church in the South Island, 25% of total attenders go to one of these two churches. This is exactly the phenomenon that has been observed in the USA, except there the very large church would be considerably bigger.[3]

Robertson predicts that more and more people will exit the smaller churches and join a large church. George Barna, the American researcher, begs to differ and predicts that the future belongs to the micro-churches:

> As I have tracked people's inclinations through our national research studies, I have concluded that by the year 2025, the spiritual profile of the nation will be dramatically different. Specifically, I expect that only about one-third of the population will rely upon a local congregation as the primary or exclusive means for experiencing and expressing their faith; one-third will do so through alternative forms of a faith-based community; and one-third will realize their faith through the media, the arts, and other cultural institutions.[4]

Barna is adamant that, 15 years from now, the majority church model will be that of small missional entities. Another devotee put it this way:

> Imagine you take two elephants and for our purposes they are a male and a female and you put them in that room behind us. You give them plenty to eat and drink and you shut the door on them. Three years later, you come back and open the door. What comes out? In three years, Mom and Dad elephant have had one baby! Now, instead of two elephants, let's pretend you put two rabbits in the room. At the end of three years, when you open the door, you had better run for your life, because millions of rabbits will explode out of that door.[5]

For about a year, my sympathies were with the micro-church movement but I soon came to see that the choice between mega-churches and smaller churches was in fact a false choice. Size was not the variable that determined whether or not a church would do daring discipleship in difficult places. I then began to wonder if Ed Stetzer[6] was closer to the mark in his delineation of three camps:

1. *The Relevants.* These are often traditional, reformed, conservatively theological folk who are simply trying to make the message of Christ, their worship and outreach more contextual and relevant.

2. *The Reconstructionists.* For this group it's not just about tweaking messages and music; it's also about deconstructing structure. They reject the organisational model and embrace more informal organic incarnational models. In my language, if megachurches are like malls and alt-churches theatres; then Reconstructionists liken the church to a tent. Their impulse is to keep it simple so it can be sent wherever and be pitched amongst whomever. Jim Belcher in his recent book *Deep Church*[7] places Australians Michael Frost and Alan Hirsch within the Reconstructionist camp.

3. *The Revisionists.* Stetzer notes that Revisionists are "questioning (and in some cases denying) issues like the nature of the substitutionary atonement, the reality of hell, the complimentarian nature of gender, and the nature of the Gospel itself".[8] Jim Belcher names Brian McLaren in their number[9] and by way of clarification states that their epistemology is very much "influenced by postmodernism".[10]

Large and smaller churches fall within each of these three camps. My history would tend to place me alongside Frost and Hirsch in the Reconstructionist camp but, to be honest, I could not sign up and fight on behalf of any of Stetzer's three camps. I have not quite deserted the ecclesiological war but for now have decided to approach the battle on quite a different front.

Evangelising the Church

The reason why our churches are in such trouble is not because they're micro or macro, relevant or not yet reconstructed or revised. The issue, as I now see it, is that many church members are not actually Christian. There, I have said it!

Our pews are populated with well-meaning but half-evangelised folk. Not surprisingly, when push comes to shove and radical discipleship and mission are called for, there is a muted response. The majority are still on a journey of faith without actually being in the faith.

Allow me another autobiographical moment. I was invited to address a conference of about 5000 people in a New Zealand city. On the Friday evening one of the other speakers gave an "evangelistic" message, inviting people to seriously consider the joys of joining Jesus. The impression was that Jesus could keep you warm in a cold world, like an electric blanket. Hundreds came forward. But to be honest, I was pretty angry over what was said and done. I still am, because that night the gospel wasn't announced.

They didn't really get to hear that a "transcendent reality had entered history"[11] and that the reign of God had invaded history in a new and dramatic way in the coming of Jesus. In the words of William Abraham, "God had moved decisively to establish his rule".[12] The promised King had come and the people needed to consider being initiated into his kingdom. They now faced a crisis of obedience. Would they pledge loyalty and follow this king and his purposes for this world? Would there now be a shift of allegiance at the core of their being that allowed for a "radical reworking, a decisive turning away from all idols"[13] so as to love God with all their hearts and love their neighbour as themselves?

The young people at this conference got a "reduced version of the gospel"[14] that said little or nothing about serious commitment. In the words of Dietrich Bonhoeffer, what they heard was "cheap grace", a gospel marked by maximum benefit and minimum obligation. I fear many of the hundred who stood that night, if they're still standing, will constitute the future church in New Zealand. If this is the case, then that church may well be anaemic and nominal, full of half-lights who have made superficial decisions. I am seriously worried that they will not step forward, put their hands up and say, "Yes, Lord, just say the word and I'll do it". A church that won't or can't do this will *crash!*

I am convinced many in our churches remain unconverted. Many, if not most, are mere assenters and attenders rather than believers or "behavers". I am not alone in this observation. Half a century ago E. Stanley Jones claimed that up to two-thirds of the church "knew little or nothing about conversion as a personal, experimental fact".[15] In the mid-1980s George Gallup, Jr. said of the church:

> We boast Christianity as our faith, but many of us have not bothered to learn the basic biblical facts of this religion. Many of us dutifully attend church, but this act appears to have made us no less likely than our unchurched brethren to engage in unethical behavior. We say we are Christians, but sometimes we do not show much love toward those who do not share our particular religious perspective. We say we rejoice in the good news that Jesus brought, but we are often strangely reluctant to share the gospel with others. In a typical day the average person stays in front of the TV set nearly 25 times longer than in prayer.[16]

Professor Ron Sider was even more damning of the church five years ago:

> Scandalous behavior is rapidly destroying American Christianity. By their daily activity, most "Christians" regularly commit treason. With their mouths they claim that Jesus is Lord, but with their actions they demonstrate allegiance to money, sex, and self-fulfillment . . . White evangelicals are the most likely people to object to neighbors of another race.[17]

Similarly, William Abraham states:

> One of the truly astonishing features of modern church life is the fact that so many church members need to be evangelized. This judgment is not offered in anger or frustration; it is a fact we record with regret. Renewal can come not by starting from scratch but by clearly understanding that Christian initiation has been partial and incomplete. Perhaps we might say that people in modem Western Christianity have been half-evangelized.[18]

Is it any wonder then that the people who fill our churches don't respond to the command to love their neighbour? I believe one reason our churches are populated by half-converts is because we've got lost in salvation and no longer appreciate what the word actually means. Conversion confusion reigns supreme. A way out of this quagmire is to grasp again: *ordo salutis*!

Ordo Salutis for Saints and the Streets

The *New Dictionary of Theology* defines *ordo salutis* as "the systematic ordering of the various elements in personal salvation".[19] N T Wright takes the phrase *ordo salutis* to mean, "the lining up in chronological sequence of the events which occur from the time when a human being is outside the community of God's people, stuck in idolatry and consequent sin, through to the time when this same erstwhile sinner is fully and finally saved".[20]

To break it down even further, *ordo salutis* outlines how the themes of regeneration, faith, repentance, justification and sanctification are related to each other. Take for example, the respective orders of salvation from John Wesley, the eighteenth-century revivalist and Tom Wright, the current Bishop of Durham:

John Wesley[21] *Via Salutis*	NT Wright[22] *Ordo Salutis*
Divine foreknowledge	Divine foreknowledge
Calling – Prevenient Grace	Calling
Regeneration	Gospel: The Kingdom of God
Awakening	Loyalty/Faith
Repentance	Vindication
Justification	Pardon
Faith	Faith
Sanctification	Works/Sanctification
Justification According to Works	Judgment According to Works
Glorification	Glorification

Convinced of the need to recapture an order of salvation, I have begun to formulate what I believe is a theologically sound and missiologically effective approach.

Divine foreknowledge
Calling to those Asleep
Awakening
Searching
Awareness
Striving
Announcement
Loyalty
Acceptance
Baptism
Assembly
Works
Attainment

This order may be approached via horizontal and vertical streams (see below). Essentially, though not exclusively, the horizontal terms are a commentary on human activity and response where God is still at work. The vertical dimensions are essentially about divine activity. Rather than creating dualism, my intention in separating the two is purely for the purposes of clear communication.

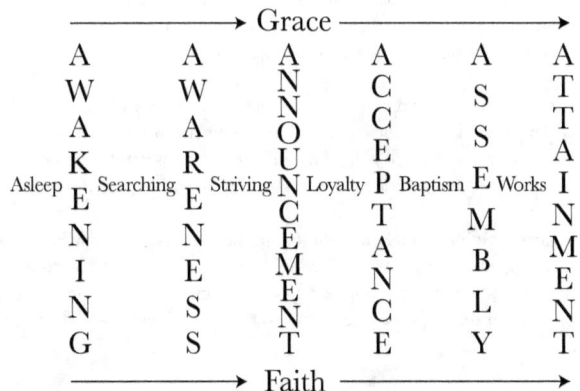

Each part of this order of salvation deserves careful biblical and theological definition. I will only attempt an introductory working definition.

- *Foreknowledge*: A God who takes initiative. The old arguments over predestination and whether or not God only comes to those he has elected to be saved are not a concern of this lecture. What is important is that God comes to us freely and out of love and generosity.

- *Calling to Those Asleep*: God comes to those John Wesley describes as being in a "state of sleep",[23] and who are unaware of their need for him. In this sleep-like state a person may feel at rest, secure, and enjoy a "kind of peace . . . and a kind of joy".[24]

- *Awakening*: This is the wake-up call. Depending on the person and their circumstances, this can be sudden, like that of an alarm bell; or quiet and gradual. It may come gradually or in the form of a crisis. Either way the person begins to sense that there are other realities in life apart from those that they have become used to in their sleep-walking state.

- *Searching*: A human response to "awakening" is that of seeking or searching for what these other realities might be. This search may take someone, for example, into the drug world, occultism, meditation or other areas looking for revelation. The sociologist Robert Wuthnow describes seekers wandering in the hills looking for someone or something, and in their investigative search picking and choosing from all sorts of places and traditions.[25] Bill Hybels, pastor of Willow Creek Church, makes a plea for the wider church to be sensitive to these seekers.[26]

- *Awareness*: In this searching some actually end up finding themselves. Like the prodigal son in his far-off place, they come to themselves.[27] There is a turning from one view of self to a different view which may include seeing oneself as fundamentally flawed. Without necessarily knowing the language of Zion, a person sees and experiences themselves as being sick to the core.[28]

- *Striving*: A new self-awareness of something being terribly wrong with self can result in a determined effort for change. This might mean changing friends, locations, jobs or signing up for self-help courses. These actions can be likened to the "fruits of repentance" as mentioned by John the Baptist in Scripture.[29]

- *Announcement*: God reveals himself to the person. The God who has acted with convincing grace now acts with saving grace. Jesus is revealed as King and Healer. The gospel is the inauguration of a new kingdom with a new king, who favours his people rather than opposes them, and comes to pardon them and bring power over sin.

- *Loyalty*: Acceptance of King Jesus is demonstrated by submission and a pledge of loyalty or faithfulness to his kingdom and purposes. Those who do so, entrust themselves to God's view, placing themselves on his side.

- *Acceptance*: Through the pledge of allegiance to the king, God declares that we are right. He pardons us and we experience the assurance of now being a child and servant of the king.

- *Baptism and Assembly*: There is an initiation into the body of Christ, an entering in to the new Israel of God. Costly discipleship is no solo affair. It is done with others. The church also instructs the new believer in the creeds, gifts of the Spirit and spiritual disciplines needed for effective service.

- *Works and Mission*: The expression of loving mercy, doing justice, loving our neighbours and active evangelism: word and deed, proclamation and demonstration.

- *Attainment*: On that day at the end of time, we will be called to give an account of how we as loyal subjects lived our days and nights. More specifically we will be asked what we did to the "least" in our midst.[30]

Let us be clear. To have an emotional crisis or spiritual experience (awakening) does not make you a Christian. To be on a journey of faith (searching) or even accepting that you are flawed by sin (awareness) is still some distance from becoming a Christian. To be sincere in wanting to change and doing all that can be done on this front (striving) is still a different place to that of being a Christian. Even believing in Christ as King, does not necessarily locate you in the new Israel of God. Even the Devil knows and believes these things.

It is my view that many in our churches, having arrived at any one of these "landing places", have become convinced they are Christians. The reality is that they still have not reached the place of loyalty or received all that Christ offers. They are caught in a kind of anaemia, characterised by a nominal and superficial approach to the Christian call. Some are half-way and are yet to shine fully from that half-lit place. They have yet to count the cost of following a crucified Lord.

My fear is that these "half-lights" soon may comprise a critical mass in the church. The urgent, exciting, and tricky task of our times then is to evangelise the church! We must dare to become someone we never thought we could be. We must morph into evangelists, not just to the lost "out there" but to the lost in the midst of our churches.

Objections and Rejections

I suspect this kind of conversion mapping is rarely undertaken, certainly *ordo salutis* is rarely mentioned in churches today. Perhaps it has been amputated from the Body as if it were an archaic and now useless appendage.

There are clearly strong objections from some quarters. There are those who claim that placing doubts in the minds of those who assume they already qualify as Christians is judgmental and contributes to conversion confusion. I sympathise, but this interpretation does not fit with what I am proposing. The *ordo salutis* does not dismiss the journey people are on. It simply helps them discern where they are placed on the pathway of faith. This revelation is not imposed. Rather than condemnation it should be seen as a cause for celebration and a reminder that there is still distance to travel.

There are also those who would object on the grounds that establishing a "way of salvation" smacks of an overly formulaic and hegemonic approach. Implicit is the idea that everyone must pattern their journey of faith logically and chronologically. Even though there are discrete steps, Randy Maddox reminds us that this order is more of a "continuing journey into increasing depths of grace upon grace".[31] Therefore, far from all having to go through a sausage machine in a linear fashion, *ordo salutis* is about each person developing a responsive and ever deepening relationship with God.

It must also be noted that I chose to use bullet points rather than numbers to pinpoint the landing places. In other words, this spectrum, pathway or *ordo salutis* does not infer that everyone must go through all of these places or follow the sequence given. Some may receive "the bad news" by experiencing themselves as flawed and then welcome Jesus as "the good news". Finally they have found the Great Physician who can cure them of their sin sickness. Others may first encounter Jesus and his call on their life (the good news) and then become convinced that they don't have it in themselves to fulfil that call (the bad news).[32]

Another objection is that *ordo salutis* appears very anthropocentric and not theocentric. In other words, we run the risk of suggesting that God's entire enterprise revolves around us and is about us and our salvation. N T Wright has in recent decades warned against this:

> The theological equivalent of supposing that the earth goes round the sun is the belief that the whole of Christian truth is all about me and my salvation. I have read dozens of books and articles . . . on the topic of justification. Again and again the writers, from a variety of backgrounds, have assumed, taken it for granted, that the central question of all is, "What must I do to be saved?" or (Luther's way of putting it), "How can I find a gracious God?" or, "How can I enter a right relationship with God?" . . . But we are not the centre of the universe. God is not circling around us. We are circling around him. It may look, from our point of view, as though "me and my salvation" are the be-all and end-all of Christianity . . . God made humans for a purpose: not simply for themselves, not simply so that they could be in relationship with him, but so that through them, as his image-bearers, he could bring his wise, glad, fruitful order to the world.[33]

This essay endorses Wright's point. The Scriptures are not fundamentally about "me and my salvation". Rather, the entire corpus of Scripture points to something far bigger: the kingdom of God. However, that is not to say that these biblical books don't speak about me and my salvation. Wright acknowledges this and indeed provides his own *ordo salutis* (see above).

The terminology used in the order of salvation also provides a challenge for those who object to its incongruity in this modern age. If this is the case then the real issue is more about communication than content. And of course one can engage in endless debate over the actual meaning of some of those terms. For example, the theological motif of justification, which features in many orders of salvation, is rigorously debated even today. On one side is the more reformed bloc led by John Piper and on the other side is Tom Wright coming from the *New Perspectives on Paul* corner.[34] But even if it can be shown that a term has been misused or confused, the upshot needs to be one of better use rather than non-use.

A final objection that arguably comes from the emerging church, rests on the belief that the *ordo salutis* has been superseded by recent work on the theory of "bounded and centred sets". Paul Hiebert was one of the first to employ this frame. He asks, "Can an illiterate peasant, tired and hungry after a long day's work, become a Christian after hearing the gospel only once?"[35] Those who represent "becoming a Christian" as "a bounded set" insist the person be fully aware of what it means to be "in" the faith and that once "in" there is little room for further growth and change. In this set, it is nigh impossible for the aforementioned peasant to become a Christian after hearing the gospel only once.

The "centred-set option" attempts to discern whether or not the peasant is at least heading in the direction of Christ the Centre. In other words, what is most important is the relationship that the peasant has with the centre. Hiebert seems to suggest, therefore, that the peasant can become a Christian upon hearing the gospel only once, provided the peasant is heading toward the centre.

Michael Frost and Alan Hirsch have stated their preference for the centred-set approach when they write, "rather than seeing people as Christians or non-Christians, as in or out, we would see people by their degree of distance from the center, Christ".[36] What matters is not the crossing of lines but movement toward or away from the centre. A person moving toward Christ the Centre then, is a person in the process of being converted.

I am not convinced by this approach. In these politically correct and overly inclusive times it seems to have a convenient vagueness. If a Buddhist attempts to imitate Christ and moves toward such a centre, does this mean that they are converted? Abraham rightly reminds us that in becoming a Christian there is not just a change in direction and relationship but also "the adoption of a particular theological vision and the appropriation of a specific moral orientation".[37] It seems to me that the centred-set approach borders on collapsing the Christian faith into a type of salvation by good works whereby a person is a Christian by virtue of their authenticity, imitation of Christ's works and sincerity.

Ordo salutis plots a middle path between the bounded and centred sets. It is both directional (centred set) but also delineated (bounded set). The continuum allows for both process (centred set) and crisis (bounded set). Interestingly, Paul Hiebert, who originally proposed the bounded-centred set model, prefers neither. Rather, in his thinking on salvation, he opts for what he terms a "fuzzy" set which I think comes close to resembling the *ordo salutis*:

> If we use ratio ("fuzzy") sets to think about conversion, the picture looks different. Conversion from Hinduism to Christianity becomes a process in which the change may take place suddenly or gradually. In the transition the person can be seen as three-quarters Hindu and one-quarter Christian, half and half, one-quarter and three-quarters, and finally 100 per cent Christian.[38]

Hiebert is the first to admit a "fuzzy" set raises a new set of questions: "But is there no moment of salvation? Can a person serve Hindu gods and Christ at the same time? We who look from the outside may not see a point of conversion, but what about God, who looks at the heart? May it be that what appears fuzzy to us, because we cannot see into the heart, is clear to God? In missions work should we work more on drawing people to Christ and focus less on seeing salvation as a single decision and discipling as a less critical process that will somehow take care of itself?"[39]

Hiebert, in answer to these questions, writes:

> A ratio or fuzzy intrinsic-set approach to missions solves some of these problems by allowing transformation to be a process. A person may make many decisions, no one of which is decisive, but all of which, taken cumulatively, make the person a Christian. This fits our human view of things. There are people who are clearly Christians and others who are clearly not. But many seem to be in between. Moreover, many Christians report no one decision marking their conversion.[40]

The *ordo salutis* makes space for Hiebert's "in-between" ones. It recognises that people can be on a journey of faith which involves many turnings and decisions. But the *ordo salutis* also speaks of a conscious and decisive moment where an allegiance shift occurs and one declares that they now belong to a revealed king. Becoming a Christian is about a series of decisions but also a crisis of costly submission and loyalty to Christ the Ruler.

Practising the Ordo Salutis

How this works in practice is quite simple. When talking with a Sally, Steve or Vicky I simply draw the *ordo salutis*, explaining and illustrating each marker along the way. I may even use bits and pieces of my own life-story to illustrate a marker. For example, for most of my childhood I was in the "state of sleep". I was raised in a non-Christian home and had very little notion of right and wrong, true and false, good and bad.

There was one night during my final year at school that I will never forget. When I came home there was no one there. I waited until dinner-time and still no one appeared. As the hours went by it became clear I was home alone. I decided on sleep and prepared for bed. As I pulled back the covers a little white envelope fell to the floor. It was a "Dear Michael" letter from my mother, informing me she had finally decided to separate from my dad. I was devastated and confused.

Even though we weren't an especially close family I was really hurt. The pain birthed within me a question: Why was there so much inequality and suffering in the world? The following year I took this question to university where I studied social sciences. University gave me information but not much wisdom, so I left. Unable to ignore the question about suffering, I continued what was to become a life's pursuit of truth. The next few years were filled with drug use and drug dealing, vegetarianism and Eastern mysticism, either living communally or as a hermit. The letter informing me of my parent's divorce was my awakening.

The awakening took me into search mode, especially the world of drugs. There was one particular night when a number of us went to a party to "use and deal" drugs. The police raided the place and we managed a fast exit. As we roared down the road I noted that Paul, seated across from me in the back of the VW van, was reading a little red book. I asked him what it was and he simply said, a "Gideon's Bible" that he had picked up somewhere. When he handed it to me, I opened it randomly and read the words.

I had chanced upon a list which described people in the last days. They would be lovers of themselves. I gave myself a tick for that one. I also scored on being disobedient to parents. In fact, as I went through the list I found myself ticking most of them. It was then and there that I began to see I was basically "stuffed" and flawed, and that I was not only a victim but also a villain. This episode of self-awareness helped convict me over what I would now call the sins in my life and that something about me was causing these sins. I had a sense that an assassin lurked within me, intent on bringing me down. This altered view of self was a turning point.

Space does not allow me to describe also my subsequent experiments in trying to change — striving — to when I first saw Jesus as Messiah — announcement — my pledge of loyalty and assurance of his pardon — acceptance. What is important is that my awakening was not my conversion, nor was my new understanding of self, nor my attempts at change or seeing Christ as King. All of these were needed and each was to be celebrated but they did not mean I was converted. Herein lies my concern.

Too often today, when someone experiences an awakening, a self-awareness episode or even a revelation of Christ, they are declared to have become a Christian. Take Phil (not his real name) for example. He attended a church service and was quite simply blown away by a sermon and a song. He sat there stunned. As he tried to explain this experience to his Christian friends they quickly pronounced him as having had a conversion experience. He lived with this notion for several years but continued to steal and use drugs. When at last we chanced upon each other and I heard his story, I saw that things didn't quite add up. I set before him the *ordo salutis* and quickly, through his own admission, he declared that he had simply been awakened and there was now much more work to do. To cut a long story short, when I next saw him four months later I knew he was different before a word passed between us. He told me of his recent conversion and baptism. He is now exploring ways to be actively engaged in mission.

Steve (see above), also went through the *ordo salutis* with me, and concluded that he had no problems with Jesus as an example but could not accept Jesus as king and master. In other words, he had warmed to Jesus' humanity but shied away from his divinity and therefore saw no need to pledge his loyalty to the Son of God. Steve had come along way. I applauded and affirmed that, but let him see where he was stuck. This was the first time he'd been given clarity on where he was on the journey. In his church he was encouraged to see himself as a Christian, but deep down he intuitively knew he wasn't quite there.

I hazard a guess that there are many like Steve in the church today; believers of sorts but not followers. Steve acknowledged he was stuck but the reason didn't become clear until several conversations later. His reluctance to acknowledge Jesus as king had much to do with estrangement from his father who had bullied him in childhood. Steve was scared of powerful figures and had not wanted to relinquish his power again. Work still needs to be done here. While I fully appreciate his situation, I won't call Steve something he has not yet become.

In a sense, the *ordo salutis* acts as a map, helping people to locate themselves, to know where they have come from, where they are now and where to next. The merits are many:

- It is inclusive and locates most, if not all, on the page.
- Even those who are asleep are still on the page and God knows them.
- God is involved from the beginning to the end.
- There is cause for celebration no matter where a person is located.
- There is always room for forward movement. Even a settling place can be a stepping stone.
- It recognises various kinds of grace: convincing, saving and sanctifying.
- It recognises different types of faith: speculative, assent, loyalty and trusting.

Pastoral Recommendations

I would like to make a plea for:

1. A moratorium on the so-called "altar-call". Instead of asking people to come to the front and give their lives to Jesus, I suggest we invite people to put their hand up if they are interested in exploring the Christian faith further. Those who respond could be encouraged to join a small circular group for an extended period of time. There, questions and informed conversations would be encouraged with the coordinator acting, not just in the role of facilitator, but as spiritual mentor.

2. A moratorium on one person telling another that they are now a Christian. Leave time and space for the "penny to drop" and for that person to declare as a first step that they are now on God's side of things.

3. A moratorium on the CEO/manager style of pastoring in favour of theologically trained pastors becoming evangelists to their own church members. This will mean recapturing the practice of visitation and getting alongside people in their homes, workplaces or in cafes. This approach would see the pastor come alongside to assist each member of the church determine whether or not they are in fact "in" the faith.

4. Finally, encouraging training institutions to build courses on the morphology of conversion into the curriculum. Students need to get "on message", become absolutely clear what is involved in conversion and be able to differentiate and communicate the constituent parts of salvation in a way that is sincere and life-giving. We must equip our students to be evangelists to the lost in the church, to the anaemic, nominal, half-lights who have made superficial decisions. The challenge is for a new generation of students to become "physicians of the soul who can link the lost and weary with the healing medicine of the kingdom".[41]

It is my firm view that the enactment of these four recommendations will go a long way in transforming the half-lights in our churches into flames of love.

Chapter Six

HOW DIRTY ARE THE HANDS AND FEET THAT FOLLOW JESUS

JON OWEN

Peace is the fruit of love, a love that is also justice. But to grow in love requires work — hard work. And it can bring pain because it implies loss — loss of the certitudes, comforts, and hurts that shelter and define us. — Jean Vanier

We exist in interesting times, not only as the people of God, but also in the scope of world history. That is seemingly a cheap and easy way to begin a lecture, however, consider this: we are all huddled together on this planet with more people currently alive than have ever existed for the entire span of human history. The axis marking where the majority of people hold to the Christian faith has begun to shift from the axis of Europe and North America to what author Philip Jenkins refers to as the global South (Africa, South America and Asia). Our attention is finally beginning to be drawn to the new, exciting and alarming expressions of faith that are either strongly established or freshly emerging from these places. The global South is where the majority of the world's poor reside, many living in slums created by the rapid urbanisation of the planet. Currently one in every six of God's children lives in a slum on this planet. This number is predicted to rise to one in every three by 2025.

I don't intend to present a socio-cultural analysis of that seismic shift with its missiological implications, though that would be fascinating, as it contains the whispers of where we need to be heading — let's leave that in the hands of far more capable people. I hope to explore the issues we will face as we seek to engage with the opportunities this brave new world presents us.

As a nation that clings to the coat-tails of what is rapidly becoming the minority — the global North — and yet is geographically located in close proximity to the emerging majority, we are presented with unique opportunities to be a vital part in helping influence, enable and equip this shift. This leaves another possibility open to us — we may even be able to pioneer what this shift implies for post-Christian nations. For nations like ours the march of economic development and secularism seem to be inseparable dance partners.

Bread and Circuses

Missionally speaking, could there be any more important issues to focus our attention? Apparently the answer is "yes". If it's any consolation, we seem to be reflecting the broader culture here, rather than calling it forward. Consider this, what do you think the No. 1 bestselling book in this nation over the past five years has been? Was it a political thriller or an analysis of our nation and future trends? No, sadly, it is neither of those, rather it is a little book called *Spotless*. Is this vital subject material? Effective housekeeping?

Surely as the body of Christ we have more important concerns? Sadly, the answer to that one seems to be "no". Recently author and famous Christian speaker Rob Bell published a book called *Love Wins*. Even before it was published it set the Twittersphere ablaze, with comments about the material receiving such a high volume of internet traffic that it trended worldwide on Twitter, reaching the Top #7 topics being tweeted upon in the world. This rarefied air is only reserved for Twitter Royalty — Justin Bieber, Lindsay Lohan and Charlie Sheen. When the body of Christ mobilises we get noticed. It's just a pity that all this traffic was generated before the book was even released. This world faces many issues that are real and require our best energy, and they require that now.

I almost wonder if that is how we have let the world get to where it is now — by attending to our households so fastidiously we simply haven't noticed the changes taking place around us. It's all a game of bread and circuses.

Unfortunately while we are busily entertaining ourselves to death we are missing our world's transition into a new era of history, one in which we must find a role or perish.

Holocaust survivor Victor Frankl suggested that, "we detect, rather than invent, our mission in life". We are now at a time which calls for more detecting than doing, more listening than talking. Unfortunately, as missionaries, this has never been our favourite position.

New Perspectives

As a young boy growing up in the Australian church through the late 70s and early 80s, talks on mission were common. The talks I sat through as an impressionable young lad were nearly always delivered by older white men, usually in horrific 70s plaid suits, talking about and showing slides of poor little brown kids through the old Kodak Carousel slide projector that sometimes would have a slide or two loaded in upside-down for good measure.

I am the only son of the seventh son of a Sri-Lankan man and his Indian wife, from stock that was for countless generations steeped in the Hindu-Buddhist traditions of our ancestors, now standing here to share with you all. My only qualification is that I have spent my entire adult Christian life in ministry amongst poor white kids in Australia's public housing ghettos.

There is something truly beautiful in that. It speaks of the global nature of our faith. No one holds the title deed for the exclusive land rights to the great commission. It is something in which we all share. As Indigenous elder, Rev. Graham Paulson once remarked in a different context, "no longer are we a mission field, but we are now a mission force".

Whilst I caricatured the missionaries in the 1970s I mean them no disrespect. Missionaries of the past era thought of ten-year stints as "short-term missions". Off they went on nothing short of heroic journeys to unknown lands amongst unfamiliar peoples whom they most certainly would never before have encountered, not knowing what the future held for their families. They don't deserve our respect, they command it.

The Emerging Majority

The image of our blondest and brightest missionaries boldly going to evangelise the "heart of darkness" is now trending the other way, with waves of Asian, African and Latin missionaries entering the "heart of whiteness" and re-energising Western churches, economies and birth rates in societies that have been drowning silently and slowly in the molasses of secularism.

The balance of people who identify themselves as followers of Jesus is shifting globally from the North to the South. By Australian standards, the average follower of Jesus is a well-heeled, university-educated person of Caucasian heritage. By global standards, however, the average follower of Jesus looks like a poor, illiterate African woman living in a slum raising seven children with no running water.

I do not for a second presume to speak for those growing up in absolute poverty. I resist the horrible childhood imperative given me by my father, "that absolutely everything that I say and do reflects on India". Representing over 1.2 billion people is a heavy burden to bear for an awkward six year old with a bad hairdo in East Keilor in 1981. I do speak not for them, but as just one small voice whose heritage is located amongst the emerging majority.

Who I am is as important as anything I have to share. I am no self-made man with unique ideas that I wish to foist upon the world. Rather as Spurgeon so eloquently stated, "I am but one beggar helping another beggar to find bread".

African Ubuntu wisdom dictates that "I am what I am because of who we all are". I am the product of a community. The only son of a seventh son of a Sri-Lankan man and his Indian wife who were "transmigrated" between British colonies. Transmigration — that's an incredibly British way of saying that they were forcibly relocated to Malaysia to displace an indigenous population. This was done so a palm oil plantation could be geared away from serving the needs of the local community and reoriented towards export. The long tentacles of the British East India Company have wrapped my family history in their long embrace.

I was not simply spat out upon these shores, bereft of any vestiges of history and culpability, and neither are you. My family history is laced with injustice, both in what was done to us and what we have done to others. Hence, I consider the story of my ancestors to be woven deeply and indelibly into the fabric of this nation.

My faith in Jesus was birthed and nurtured in Australia. I have a deep love for the body of Christ in this nation. I also have a deep respect for my ancestors and the traditional owners of this land and wish to honour them. I hope that we can detect our way into the opportunities presented to us.

We are one of the most multicultural nations on earth, with over 44 per cent of our population either born overseas or having a parent who was. Out of sheer dumb luck (or is it?) we are geographically located in the Asia-Pacific Region. This region encompasses one of the most exciting windows of Christian growth and the majority of the planet's population. We possess immense theological resources at our disposal, with Bible colleges packed with world-class theologians.

I hope to provoke a discussion, based in love, that may lead to a new way for us to engage with the issues which face our body globally. It is my prayer that we can come out from behind ourselves, and have an honest, thought-provoking discussion about what our role could be in the new world which is breaking in upon us. No longer is this a matter of whether the changes are coming. How we engage with them is all that matters now. How is our engagement going so far? I have no idea. However, let me share with you a few of my greatest mistakes in ministry so far, in the hope that my humiliation will encourage a way forward. When I say mistakes, I mean mistakes. Most of the time when lecturers say this they offer some pretty weak examples of failure. Let me reassure you, when I say that I regularly make mistakes in ministry I speak with the utmost authority and integrity!

Messing Up

The neighbourhood in which my wife and I minister is located in the heart of one of Australia's largest public housing estates. The 2770 postcode also has within it, to the surprise of many, the largest number of Indigneous Australians of any postcode in Australia. For a young couple interested in the issues of shalom justice amongst the marginalised, this presented us with a wonderful opportunity for personal engagement with an issue that affects us as a nation.

The litmus test of whether an issue qualifies as one of national importance is if it causes an argument at the dinner table — then it is counts. This immediately rules in topics like asylum seekers, Aboriginal peoples and Azaria Chamberlain's disappearance.

We met with some local Indigenous leaders and began to build a relationship that quickly led to some opportunities for us to minister under them, or so I thought at the time. This relationship continued for a few years and more than a few observers marvelled at the levels of partnership and cooperation which we had achieved in such a short time, levels that many groups had never attained after many years.

Then disaster struck. Through a series of miscommunications and errors, what began as a small issue soon escalated. Right in the middle of this an external tragedy struck the community and that was enough to exacerbate an already strained relationship. The working relationship ceased shortly afterwards. I was gutted. If anyone could make it work, it would have been me. Pride had gotten the better of me. I had always told myself that this was going to work precisely because I was not a white face, that I was making a difference because I was from the same side of the colour ledger as them. So I took the basics for granted.

Mea Culpa, Mea Culpa, Mea Maxima Culpa

What had brought me down here were pride and power. The former caused me to overestimate what was being accomplished and neglect attending to the small issues, which led to me taking certain elements of our relationship for granted; and the latter I underestimated. The most dangerous forms of power are the ones which go unrecognised by the one who wields them. A misunderstanding of my own perceived power damaged a once rocky but relatively strong relationship which we are slowly in the process of rebuilding.

I made a fatal error. I mistook the gathering of the correct information for the long and arduous journey of transformation. I also fell into the trap of contemporary Western training: that engagement can somehow occur outside the bounds of a deep and committed relationship. That sounds so elementary, so basic. Yet we know that for a relationship to be deep and committed it must move from being shallow and polite. The only way this happens is through conflict, is it not? Still to this day there are certain sections of the community where I now walk with a deservedly tarnished image.

Even More Messing Up

The second story occurred when a young girl in our neighbourhood became homeless after years of abuse from family members. She had to make a break, she was sick of "couch surfing" — which for a teenage girl in our neighbourhood is more about giving than receiving. When we were approached by a close friend and community leader who asked if we would consider taking her in, Lisa and I immediately agreed. Care for the most vulnerable has never merely been an aspirational value for my wife. Christ's love and compassion are meaningless for her if they are not practically and tangibly lived out in the messiness of everyday life.

To describe the year she lived with us as challenging would be an understatement. This was the year I experienced my first panic attack. This occurred around the time that we heard about some terrible rumours. Our community understands events through the cultural categories with which they are familiar. To the outside observer there is nothing unusual about a young girl moving in with a family. A family is a "safe" place. However, what this means in our community is that daddy is getting a little bit on the side, from the comfort and convenience of his own home. How could I have been so naive as to think the same rumours would not spread around the community about me?

Again, I walked around our community with my head bowed carrying around a very tarnished image. All my hopes and dreams for ministry lay shattered in the dirt at my feet. My tears soon turned them into mud. My mother never told me there would be years like this! I mean I knew all the theory, I'd read the books, listened to the talks, I'd seen the movie — yet still stuffed it up.

What Was Happening?

Before we moved into Mt Druitt, Lisa and I visited a local family we had some connection with from Melbourne. When they heard about what we were hoping to do they exchanged sideways glances. "I'll give you 18 months tops before you leave, it is too hard here for that", offered the father.

Why is that? The answer we have found is that what happened to us pretty much happens to everyone who wants to minister here. Eventually their good name and reputation get smeared with dirt. It is usually at this point in their exasperation and exhaustion they pull up stumps and run. It is the "honourable" thing to do. No longer is their involvement on their terms. The power has shifted through rumours and innuendo, and they burn out. No longer can they minister on their own terms. My community is littered with the corpses of good-hearted and well-intentioned ministers.

Poor and marginalised communities have a rhythm and tempo all of their own and, if it isn't picked up on, you will be dancing out of step. If you enter, as I did, with a messiah complex, you will be wounded, perhaps even mortally so. What I needed was not better missiology, but a better spirituality. I desperately required a spirituality of engagement which could build resilience in myself. We need one that can sustain institutions and individuals. One that comforts, holds, sustains and nurtures, but also pushes us back out onto the front lines. Can Jesus provide this?

Where to from Here?

Samuel Johnson reminds us that we "need to be reminded more often than we need to be instructed". I contend that re-examining Jesus as a model for mission will help show us the way into engaging with this new world.

We need look no further than Jesus. However, we need to recover Jesus away from the domesticated model that far too many of us had handed down to us in our childhood. We have inherited a far too mild picture of Jesus. Why is a good, healthy understanding of Jesus important for missional engagement amongst the poor and marginalised? Because how we view Jesus will determine our response not only to him, but also to our world and our brothers and sisters.

The Importance of a Robust Christology for Missiology

Jesus never asked to be worshipped, only to be followed. Now, worship is a natural and extremely important response to Christ, but I will be exploring Christ's example, his humanity, not his divinity. This of course does not exclude the latter. We need to rediscover who Jesus really was. I offer you a small story to illustrate the importance of this point. Thirty years ago a very courageous young man moved into the neighbourhood where I now minister. He was moved to the most notorious block of housing at a tumultuous time. He began to minister to his neighbours in amazing ways. He was from a Pentecostal background and used this empowerment to give him the strength to minister — and minister he did. Some amazing things happened through him, including rescuing women and children from situations of abuse and delivering some from the demons of addiction. His house was regularly filled with the homeless. He truly was in the thick of it all.

One day some children were arguing near his front yard over an impromptu cricket match. This escalated to the point where one of the fathers marched up to the other protagonist's father (his best friend), held a shotgun to his temple, and pulled the trigger. The minister was first on the scene and was the one who mopped up brains from the floor of the fibro townhouse while police arrested the shooter. This minister was faithful and committed to his call.

One of the platforms for his faith that kept him going was his unswerving belief that Jesus was powerful and hence offered him and his family powerful protection, as his protection rests over the faithful. This reassurance was sadly soon to end. In the midst of the hustle and bustle of life, one night he was attacked and beaten up by a man he had ministered to for a few years. For him this was the beginning of the end.

If you track his brutally honest and haunting memoirs written in the book, *Peacemaker in Cement City* (self-published), he was never the same. From that moment on he was assailed with doubts and fears, often lamenting, "How could Jesus allow that to happen to me?" He simply could not assimilate the experience he had with what he had been taught to believe was true of Jesus.

With this central pillar of his understanding of Jesus removed, the cognitive dissonance grew too big and, while he continued to minister, he began to burn out. This eventually led to a series of health problems which gave way to a physical and emotional breakdown. He still lives in our neighbourhood. His health required him to be transferred to a quieter street where he still ministers to children. I do not offer this story to run this man down. He has stood in places for Jesus where many would never dare go. I offer this story to say that how he viewed Jesus matters and mattered enormously. In his case we can see where it led.

What about You?

When we reduce Jesus' exclusive concern to the next world we reduce him to little more than a ticket vendor offering entry to a platonic heaven. This strips from him a concern for our world. This leaves him with nothing to say about the issues which threaten our world now; issues which affect the lives of the world's poorest here and now — a universal and central concern of the global South where the world's poorest are found. If we respond to these needs these are seen as natural concerns that, at best, are humanist ideals, normally are not considered part of the "essential gospel" and, at worst, are leading people down a path of religion apparently based upon "works". If this is our view of Jesus then he holds little hope for a hurting world, other than its extinction.

In the current milieu, we no longer seek Jesus, we strive for Jesus and create a subtle form of "works–based" religion. It quickly descends into a worthiness game. We become obsessed with who is in and who is out. We strive to be worthy. We pursue a spirituality based upon achievement, perfection and excellence. Go to any church website and browse the titles of their last few months of sermons and you'll quickly see what I mean. This soon leads to association only with those who are in pursuit of the same dream. It is in this context that we entertain notions that Jesus is a cosmic protector who blesses the faithful with protection and prosperity.

I always imagine what excellence would look like for the single mothers who live in public housing estates across our nation and I am often reduced to tears. True engagement at the margins needs to be flavoured by the radical grace that Christ extends to all of creation.

The obsession with personal development has another unintended side-effect. It leads its adherents down the smooth path of a spirituality of detachment — "this world is not my home, I'm just passing through". This, to put it quite bluntly, is not the Christian vision. It fits far more comfortably with the practices associated with the Theravada Buddhist practices of my ancestors than it does with those in pursuit of Christianity. Following Jesus is a messy business. You don't escape this life without scars. Jesus certainly didn't.

If we are to be something more than a sidebar in what God is doing in the world we need to join with the courageous groups who are moving back to a spirituality which is based upon a Jesus who embodies grace, engagement and risk. Do we have a model in Jesus that helps us on our way? Are we seeking to remake him in our image for our own convenience? If we examine the contours of the life of Jesus we find no better path back. His life does not conform comfortably within the constraints which we have attempted to place upon him.

Jesus in the Gospel of Mark Chapter One

The most common image many people have of Jesus is one of a gentle shepherd, surrounded by children and sheep. This is not too dissimilar to the Jesus that Ricky Bobby prays to in the movie *Talladega Nights*: "Sweet baby Jesus all cute and cuddly in his golden fleece nappies, hasn't even uttered a word yet . . .". You get the picture. The other image held by many is one of a passive man who wasn't fully present to the moment, existing on another plane, who couldn't even speak up for himself at his trial which led to his death.

For those who know nothing about Jesus those are understandable images. Yet for this to be any kind of working image for those of us who share life with him is unacceptable.

We have been formed in an age which idealises strength, power and victorious conquests. Hence, many like their Jesus strong and victorious, regularly citing passages from Revelation to inform their image of him. Alternatives are not tolerated, being denigrated as sissy and weak. To this picture the Gospels are an affront as they depict the weaknesses, heartbreak and vulnerabilities that Jesus experienced. It is tempting to abandon the quest to be formed in the image of Jesus and instead allow Jesus to be formed in the image of the victorious, all-conquering king.

Neither should followers of Jesus base their conceptual image of him from a surface skim-reading of the Gospel of John, from which many have mistakenly formed the view that Jesus was ethereal and detached, almost floating a few inches above the ground whilst he was here. Jesus had feet and they got dirty. Our pursuit will certainly not leave us with a "Spotless" Jesus. The Jesus we find in Scripture is a fascinating character. A man with many dimensions and moods, some of them dark as well as light, tenderness balanced with confrontation. We find him sometimes angry and engaged, and at other times desolate and withdrawn.

Insights about Jesus come coupled with responsibilities to respond. We are reminded by the South American theologian Sergio Torres that "the first act of theology is commitment". To this let me add, the "first act of missiology is commitment". The insights we gain are not for our own amusement or power, they are a gift from God to be used in the service and extension of the "realm of his Lordship and grace" or kingdom, for want of a less over-prescribed label. I truly affirm Luther's "*Soli Deo Gloria*".

Where Jesus Went

Fairly early on in the piece we can discern a distinctive pattern about the places Jesus walked. His footsteps tended to move in a direction that made his peers decidedly uncomfortable - towards the outcasts. Our political leaders have the ability to run entire election campaigns based upon which of them can exclude these sections of our community the most effectively. Yet Jesus always treated them face to face and with respect. How we respond to issues such as asylum seekers in our region matters! We are a nation that is plagued with a diversity of opinion, but a paucity of experiences. The eyes of the global South are upon us. How we respond to the most vulnerable in our region not only matters, it is a matter of concern for our region.

Early on in the Gospel of Mark we find Jesus on his "campaign", coming face to face with a man suffering from leprosy. From the moment a person was diagnosed with leprosy they immediately became *persona non grata*. In Jesus' world there was scant opportunity for social mobility. You basically stayed in the position you were born in. If you were born into debt and servitude then you most likely stayed there. If you were a "lucky" slave you may become a "freedman" — released from servitude — but there wasn't much luck around back then. We live in a world with very little opportunity for social mobility too. What does Jesus do? Jesus so far has come across as authoritative, drawing his power from a source other than the approval of men. Up to this point he has also appeared to be in control, gaining respect through his healings. We have seen him moving freely between the sanctuary and the street, and up to now he was in control of this process.

That's All about to Change

We see the man with leprosy approach Jesus. On his knees he begs — if Jesus is willing, he can make him clean. Up until now the text has only hinted at the emotions of Jesus, but here we are directly told for the first time what is going on inside of him.

What is the first thing we are told? Jesus is moved with compassion. He was moved at a gut level. This is not pity or sympathy, but a stirring from deep within. Stirred from the depths, Jesus not only heals the man, but reaches out his hand and touches him. In Jesus we see the *missio Dei* enfleshed. To us this touch doesn't seem like much, but this act strips Jesus of social power and control.

Glory and Consequence

Contact with lepers has consequences. Jesus was now rendered ceremonially unclean, requiring him to undergo a period of exclusion before he could re-engage with the community. Jesus would have been very aware of this, and yet still he touched the man.

After healing the man, Jesus sends him back into the centre of town, where the socially powerful live, while he must remain on the outer. This healing has cost him. We need to meditate on that fact a little longer. Many readers and scholars have leapt too quickly to the assumption that Jesus intentionally decided that he could not openly enter towns because this healing would have made him too popular. While he never trusted crowds, Jesus was regularly found amongst them. Instead, Jesus largely remained outside towns, in the very places that people with leprosy had to reside.

If his initial contact made him an outcast then the same will certainly be true for us. If we go to those who are on the margins of society and are moved with compassion that elicits a bodily response from us, then we too will be on the slow path to becoming a social pariah.

My engagement with the poor has left me a changed man. Jesus modelled a radical engagement with the pain of this world. He didn't try to hide his face from the suffering of this world. He reassured us that he only did that which he saw his Father doing, and was always led by the Spirit and discerned the Spirit's leading. I can only do the same. These interactions weren't aberrations either; they were invitations to his followers to do likewise.

"Where you stand determines what you see."

This engagement involves moving towards the suffering in this world: seeking out the rejected and despised and hearing their cries. This will involve treating others with the same respect and dignity that Jesus treated those outside his immediate socio-cultural circle.

As followers of Jesus we will never make poverty history until we make it personal. It will involve using our networks to lobby and advocate for greater justice in the world. It will demand every ounce of our strength. Our influence will grow from our relationships and connections and the ability to persevere in the face of misunderstanding and conflict. This is a muddy path, but I believe it to be the only one available to us if we desire to change the world to be in line with values of the realm of God's lordship and grace. This is not a place where the poor are raised up and the mighty are thrown down, but where, as Aboriginal theologian Billy Williams says, "a place where we put the rightful ruler on the throne and we worship him together as sisters and brothers". This will not only give us a voice and role in the global South, it will also give us a spirituality that will help us engage with the region in a transformative relationship.

Conclusion

I think we have completely misunderstood where the true source of true spiritual and moral authority is located. We have mistakenly sought it in the heavens amongst the powerful. We have sought to "curry favour with kings", forming political alliances hoping that real influence can be found amongst them. This will be given short shrift by the global South for whom poverty is an everyday reality. Dare we ask for a more dangerous example of how this power can be misused so flagrantly than when a twit tweets a gospel of division and hatred against others and — despite supposed "well meaning" retractions — damages the marginalised. It shows this path to be a false source of power and authority. Where does true authority lie?

While many like to stand up for those living in poverty, there are too few who want to stand with them. Yet this has to be a key to following Jesus in our world. True spiritual power can be found in mud, amongst the world's pain, derision and suffering. It is in these places that we will find Jesus, beckoning us with a smile and a muddied hand. If we seek to engage with the global South will we persevere through misunderstanding and miscommunications, or will we cut and run when it gets difficult? Or will we rediscover a spirituality of place and stability to stay and usher in the New Jerusalem together?

Chapter Seven

EVERYDAY THEOLOGY IN THE iWORLD

JUSTINE TOH

In the near future we'll only be able to communicate through devices. Actual human contact will be outlawed by the Apple iCourt. — *Jim Carrey*

Apple's iconic iPod advertisements summarise the spirit of the age, and the dreams and aspirations of the world in which we live. In this world, nothing is more important than being free to be me, to be an autonomous, self-expressed individual. We can see such qualities celebrated in these silhouetted figures who are free to move any way that they wish.

Taking his cue from Apple products — all with their prefix of "i" — Dale Kuehne names this world the "iWorld".[1] It's a world committed to the freedom of the individual (the "i" of the term) to forge their own path in the world, free from the strictures of the past "tWorld" where tradition (the "t" of the term) reigned, along with religion, family and culture.[2]

In the tWorld, your identity was largely given to you. Your job, who you might marry, where you would live were largely predetermined. The individual stepped into a pre-existing role and they understood their place in a wider story. The tWorld placed a high priority on doing one's duty, since this was their responsibility. In contrast the iWorld individual believes the most important thing to do is follow their dreams.

Individualism is celebrated in our culture and is a product of the iWorld's insistence on individual freedom. This is clear to see in Apple's suite of products prefixed with "i", and also in the virtual deification of late Apple CEO Steve Jobs — particularly in relation to the commencement address he delivered to Stanford students in 2005. His speech resonated with individualist ideology: a commitment to individual vision, following one's inner voice rather than that of others, independence, and self-reliance. Extracts of this legendary speech have since been transformed into motivational catchphrases, particularly Jobs' exhortation for people to "Stay Hungry, Stay Foolish" when it came to following their dreams.[3]

This state of affairs should be of great interest to Christians, for the gospel faces a new raft of opportunities and challenges in the iWorld. I will be arguing for the need for an "everyday theology" that understands life in the iWorld and how the gospel speaks into it — which will be the focus of the final section. I hope you find the idea of everyday theology useful when it comes to navigating this mission (mine)field.

Everyday Theology: "faith seeking understanding"

For Kevin Vanhoozer, "everyday theology" is the biblically faithful attempt to make sense of everyday life.[4] It attempts to see everyday life "as God sees it and, with God's help, to be an agent of redemptive change".[5] Everyday theology is an activity of cultural exegesis that is centrally concerned with identifying and understanding the *values* communicated in the stuff of everyday life, and how we are persuaded to adopt them. With this understanding, everyday theology points to how we might live with eternity in mind instead.[6]

Everyday theology takes as a given that the gospel changes the way we view life. The Apostle Paul wrote to the Roman church that they were no longer to "conform to the pattern of this world, but be transformed by the renewing of [their] mind[s]" (Romans 12:2). Such non-conformity to the "pattern of this world" and the renewal of our minds and lives are the goals of everyday theology, for it implicitly understands that our culture shapes us into particular kinds of people, with values, attitudes and beliefs that may be out of step with the gospel. Therefore, it is important to identify such values and, by God's grace, see how we might choose differently.

Everyday theology focuses on the stuff of everyday life, because this reveals the ways that we are in the (i)World. Vanhoozer writes that "every part of life signifies something about the values and beliefs that shape culture".[7] Put another way, the stuff of our everyday life tells us stories about who we are and the nature of the world we live in — particularly what it values, and what it dismisses or ignores. These cultural stories help us answer big questions like "What's the good life?", "What should I strive for?", "Who am I?" and "Who should I be?" So, anytime in this talk when we look at examples from our culture, listen out for what they reveal about the iWorld in which we live.

That everyday theology will seek to take the gospel directly to these questions reveals the importance of contextualisation. The gospel needs to be couched in terms that are meaningful to the people being ministered to. The everyday theologian, therefore, has to be doubly skilled: not only able to read and decipher the cultural text "but also the culture of the hearers".[8] In order to do that effectively, one has to keep an ear close to the ground so as to listen out for people's fears, hopes, drives and dreams. This practice draws on theologian Paul Tillich's counsel that the best way to understand a culture or even an era is to discover its greatest anxiety and greatest hope.[9] In the end, everyday theology is all about understanding what's important to people, and bringing the gospel to bear on that. Now, let us explore the iWorld mission field in further detail.

The Mission Field of the iWorld

A good way to understand the preoccupations of the iWorld is to focus on those who have grown up in it. I'm not trying to single out young people for criticism. Rather, I want to work out what story/ies their assumptions, values and taken-for-granted ideas about themselves and the world tell us about life in the iWorld today. So while we look at young people's experience in more detail in this section, it's only because they offer — in a concentrated form — a good insight into the aspirations of the iWorld.

It's unsurprising that an iWorld obsessed with individual freedom would produce a demographic dubbed "Generation Me". That's psychologist Jean Twenge's collective term for those born from the 1970s to 1990s (which includes herself), so her analysis takes in the latter part of Generation X — roughly 1965–1979 — and all of Generation Y — roughly 1980–1994. Her book, *Generation Me: Why Today's Young Americans Are More Confident, Assertive, Entitled, and More Miserable Than Ever Before* (2006), surveys the attitudes and beliefs of young people today (and yes, her rambling subtitle effectively sums up her thesis).

The "language of the self", Twenge writes, is Generation Me's "native tongue", with the individual feeling good about themselves and focusing on their needs both high on their priorities.[10] Some broad beliefs of this generation are that people should follow their dreams, do what makes them happy, and not bother themselves with what other people think.[11] They insist on being individuals and being free to be themselves. For Generation Me, jobs are more than ways to earn a living, and should be lifestyle options inasmuch as they express the individual's identity.[12] Twenge notes the high optimism of Generation Me, who expect to go to college, make lots of money, and maybe even be famous.[13] No wonder Steve Jobs is their hero.

Perhaps a way to summarise the priorities of Generation Me — and, more broadly, the iWorld — is through the notion of mobility. Recall those iPod dancers: their freedom of movement, their hyper-flexibility and skill. These talented dancers don't just symbolise the iPod's promise of music freedom, but the expansive possibilities of the self — particularly in an iWorld dedicated to individual freedom. Mobility, then, isn't just about being able to physically move, but is about having options, opportunities and aspirations. Such a desire for mobility isn't simply confined to Generation Me, but is a general feature of the iWorld.

The iWorld's commitment to individual mobility overrides any other competing claims on the self. As such, it implicitly rejects the idea of restricting individual freedom. This attitude is artfully explored in Jason Reitman's comedy *Up in the Air* (2009) where Ryan Bingham — played by George Clooney — works for a company that specialises in firing people from their jobs. Such work means that Ryan spends most of his year flying around the country letting people go — and with the 2008–2009 Global Financial Crisis forming the backdrop of the film, it's boom time for his organisation — but Ryan wouldn't want it any other way. He loves being on the road, and even moonlights as a motivational speaker who counsels people to fit their life into a backpack and not be weighed down by relationships or possessions. "The slower we move, the faster we die", Ryan intones, "moving is living."

Up in the Air offers a snapshot of life in the contemporary West where commitment is studiously avoided because it is seen to limit individual potential and restrict people's freedom. The alternative, then, is to be perennially on the go, and this is well emphasised in the film's many shots of Ryan navigating airports and staying in impersonal hotel rooms. For him, temporariness and mobility are a desired way of life.

But maybe not just for Ryan in *Up in the Air*. Observing that modern life is one that is constantly on the go, cultural critic Richard Sennett claims that the airport waiting lounge is the architectural emblem of the contemporary era.[14] Full of strangers waiting to take off to their varied destinations, in the departure lounge all social interactions are temporary and fleeting, because no one has any intention of staying or settling where they are. The picture Sennett paints of the iWorld is one of individual choice and endless mobility, and is a sharp contrast to the tWorld that firmly rooted our lives and identities.

The transitory nature of life in the modern West also prompts the Polish sociologist Zygmunt Bauman to consider tourism as a metaphor for modern life. Like tourists, the lives of liberated Westerners are marked, Bauman says, by mobility and impermanence, a looseness of ties to place and people. The mobility of the tourist, Bauman claims, gives rise to "grazing behaviour": an endless sampling of experience that shies away from strict commitment to any one style, ideology or belief.[15] This applies as much to the physical mobility of Westerners — perhaps when they travel abroad to foreign countries — as it does to their pursuit of individual identity. Because, in contrast to the past tWorld where individual identity was shaped by one's place in a defined order, there is now "no lifelong identity" that one takes up at birth. Rather, there is a constant "living from one moment to another, living for the moment" and being the person that the present situation calls for at any given interval.[16]

Closely bound up with the iWorld's priority of individual freedom is its commitment to individual self-development. As Kuehne notes, the iWorld is "continually encouraging us to be ourselves, find ourselves, or create ourselves".[17] The idea is that people shouldn't feel limited by their circumstances, but seek to develop themselves to their fullest potential. The good life, in these terms, is one of self-actualisation and, as Oprah would put it, "Liv[ing] Your Best Life". That the "best life" or "good life" is bound up with the active pursuit of personal health, comfort, prosperity, enjoyment and satisfaction shows the pervasive nature of the therapeutic ethos in the iWorld.[18]

The therapeutic ethos is not new to the iWorld or Generation Me, but represents the full flowering of modernity's placing of the individual, not God, at the centre of cosmic meaning and purpose. A consequence of this radical reordering was that eternity receded from view as people sought the good life here on earth. Accordingly, the therapeutic ethos became a secular replacement for traditional religion as early twentieth-century Protestant values of salvation, hard work and self-denial gave way to "a therapeutic ethos stressing self-realisation in this world".[19]

Consequently, focus shifted from the "soul" — with its increasingly outmoded associations with immortality — to the satisfyingly secular "self".[20] And consumerism offered itself as the path to secular self-realisation.[21]

Let's look briefly at each in turn, for they find unique expression in the iWorld.

1. *Self not Soul*

Hiebert observes that "the only story many modern people feel a part of is their own".[22] Postmodern scepticism of grand narratives and the waning of influence of religion and tradition mean that our own personal stories become more compelling, and we look to our individual life biographies in order to provide us with a sense of meaning and significance. Self-identity, in this context, is "a reflexively organised endeavour", or the product of considered reflection.[23] It is less about one's personal characteristics and more about keeping the *story* of one's life going, and continuously revising it at will.

The iWorld exhorts us all to be centrally concerned with crafting our own identities for ourselves, without much look-in from tWorld sources of authority like religion and tradition. Moreover, the therapeutic emphasis on individual happiness and wellbeing sets the standard for many of our ideas about what it means to lead a "good life". But what does this mean for iWorld citizens who happen to be religious — and feel pulled in either direction when it comes to their allegiances: do they serve God, or serve themselves and their own happiness?

According to sociologist Christian Smith, many young American Christians today resolve this contradiction via their engagement with moral therapeutic deism.[24] This belief system is "moral" because for young believers, religion is primarily about being good and helping someone to become "a better person".[25] It's also "therapeutic" because God wants people to be happy, and to feel good about their lives.[26] This belief positions God as like a cosmic therapist or counsellor who is there when you need him but doesn't make any demands on us and doesn't really get involved — the deistic component of this belief system.[27]

This therapeutic God scarcely resembles the God of orthodox Christian belief. Moral therapeutic deism drains Christianity of sin, the need for repentance, sacrifice and humility, and makes it into a feel-good religion that prioritises personal comfort, psychological support, and emotional wellbeing. Of course, religion has typically provided such beneficial side effects, but, as Smith observes, "major American religious traditions have historically been about more than helping individuals make advantageous choices and maintain good feelings".[28]

We see here a Christianity held captive to the individualistic ideology of the iWorld, and co-opted by the therapeutic mindset. In the final section, we'll explore how the notion of being called by God responds to the context of moral therapeutic deism and invites the individual to take part in God's story rather than simply their own.

2. *Consumerism and Self-realisation*

The phrase "retail therapy" suggests a therapeutic dimension to shopping: that buying stuff and spending money can help someone to feel better. But this doesn't exhaust the feel-good potential of consumerism. Indeed, consumerism promises to turn us into the best version of ourselves we can be, and so continues our therapeutic drive for healing and wholeness.

Just consider advertising. It shows us the "good life" — how we might be if we bought the advertised product. Advertising proposes to each of us, writes visual culture critic John Berger, "that we transform ourselves, or our lives, by buying something more".[29] It does this, Berger says, by showing us beautiful, happy people who have apparently been transformed through their association with the product on sale or brand being advertised. And so when we buy a product we are also buying into a desirable way of life — the "good life", in fact.

For example, Levi's recent "Go Forth" ad campaign features a number of slim, beautiful people challenging authority, swimming with sparkly clothes on, head-banging, making out with each other — all with an air of youthful insouciance. Over these images of rebellion and rugged individualism, a voice narrates Charles Bukowski's poem "The Laughing Heart". Featuring lines like "You can't beat death but / You can beat death in life, sometimes," and "You are marvellous / The gods wait to delight / In you," the poem celebrates pioneers and those who live with passion, and claims that those who dare to defy received wisdom achieve a kind of immortality through their deeds.

This ad and accompanying poem could be something of a mission statement for Generation Me, for whom identity, lifestyle and freedom are all-important — after all, your life is your life. The advertisement celebrates the Levi's jeans wearer as a free spirit, a risk-taker, an authentic individual, and someone who lives large. Who among Generation Me today wouldn't want to be regarded as a passionate, bold, uncompromising individual who stands up for themselves and lives by their own rules?

Few of us are naïve enough to believe that buying Levi's jeans will instantly make us cool like those beautiful, authentic, self-expressed people in the ad. But advertising has taught us that we can position ourselves in a favourable way through our association with brands or products that have been imbued with particular meanings. Why else would anyone want to buy a Mercedes if not for the status envy of others, inspired by the brand's association with wealth, luxury and quality engineering?

Consumerism, then, not only involves buying stuff but is something of a makeover opportunity that promises to transform us and make us into better versions of ourselves. And consumerism relies on our own desire for wholeness, success and fulfilment to spur on our therapeutic quest to change our lives. It promotes what I call a do-it-yourself (DIY) ethos in its suggestion that individuals have the power to position themselves favourably and control, to some extent, how they are viewed by others.

This DIY ethos is not confined to advertising and consumerism but proliferates throughout our contemporary makeover culture: from weight-loss programs to self-help literature, plastic surgery, university degrees that encourage you to "start your next life" by enrolling in a course, *The Biggest Loser*, *Masterchef* and so on. These texts of makeover culture encourage us to view our lives as individual projects on which we have to work so that we can construct our identity and achieve personal fulfilment.[30]

The following quote by Tiffany Hall, trainer for *The Biggest Loser*, grants us an insight into what the individual needs to do in order to work effectively on themselves. In the quote, Hall runs through the techniques she uses to encourage the contestants to push through the pain and physical exhaustion of training:

> My training sessions are like interviews: "Why are you here, what do you want to achieve, what are you feeling now?" They need to be honest. They need to admit that when they look in the mirror, they don't like what they see.[31]

Hall relies on the contestant's dissatisfaction with themselves and their bodies when she motivates their training by asking "Why are you here?" This is the first step of a successful DIY project of successful selfhood: a brutal self-assessment. Secondly, the individual needs to identify the goal they're working towards — why Hall prods, "What do you want to achieve?" Lastly, the individual needs to commit to a lot of hard work because in a makeover culture, success or failure is a matter of personal effort — a philosophy that is wholly in keeping with the iWorld's valorisation of "me". In all of this, Hall presents the idea that everything — a svelte body, better fitness, a new life — is up for grabs if the individual wants it badly enough.

When we witness the before-and-after shots of Emma Duncan, 2010 winner of *The Biggest Loser*, it's hard to fault this approach that encourages people to push past their limits in order to get great results. But what if you fail? How does life fare for the eliminated contestants on the show?

This is one of the problems with makeover culture's glorification of individual effort. Because it's up to the individual to change and improve their life — which flows out of the iWorld's unwavering belief in the power and potential of the individual — the individual has to accept all responsibility. This is great if the individual happens to succeed but failure is always haunted by the possibility that you just didn't try hard enough.

Perhaps this explains why, as Twenge's subtitle asserts, today's young Americans are more miserable than ever before. In psychologist Martin Seligman's latest book *Flourish*, he writes that not only is depression about ten times more common than it was 50 years ago, but it is increasingly affecting people at younger ages. In the 1960s, the first onset of depression was about age 30. Now, it's about 15.[32]

Rampant depression in the West seems counterintuitive given the advantages Generation Me has over earlier generations — greater freedom and mobility, medical advances, less manual labour, and sexual liberation. But the wealth of opportunity of the average iWorld citizen — particularly in relation to individual freedom — is also part of the problem. Twenge notes that a downside to our fierce independence and self-sufficiency is that "our disappointments loom large because we have nothing else to focus on".[33]

Seligman goes further, arguing in *The Optimistic Child* that depression rates rise in tandem with "the slide away from individual investment in endeavours larger than the self: God,

Nation, Family, Duty".[34] Whether Seligman knows it or not, he links the psychological implosion of the iWorld to the waning of the way the tWorld endowed people's lives with meaning by encouraging them to look beyond themselves. Not that the tWorld was perfect — in fact, many would say it enslaved the individual self in the name of the group. But the iWorld, with all its thrilling opportunities and unparalleled liberties, hasn't exactly led us to utopia either. And focusing on the self and its desires in the iWorld is its own form of slavery.

We see such a predicament in the sex-addiction drama *Shame* (2011). The film offers a toxic vision of the iWorld in which individual freedom — especially in areas relating to sex and relationships — accepts no limits. Brandon Sullivan is a successful New York executive so controlled by his sexual compulsions that he can't be emotionally, physically or sexually intimate when he tries to have a "normal" relationship with a woman he clearly likes. For Brandon, sex needs to be anonymous, casual and on demand. Not only does this isolate him from potential romantic partners but it also cuts him off from relationship with anyone who would care about him.

In some ways, *Shame*'s Brandon Sullivan recalls *American Psycho's* Patrick Bateman, though Brandon is far more agreeable than the sociopathic would-be serial killer of Bret Easton Ellis's imagination. Both Brandon and Patrick enjoy the "good life" — they are handsome, successful, well-off and live lives of unparalleled freedom — but they each tell a story of spiritual emptiness in the midst of material (*American Psycho*) and sexual (*Shame*) abundance. In a recent interview, Bret Easton Ellis reflects on his similarities to his character:

> On the surface, like Patrick Bateman, I had everything a young man could possibly want to be "happy" and yet I wasn't . . . Patrick Bateman is the extreme embodiment of that dissatisfaction. Nothing fulfils him. The more he acquires, the emptier he feels. On a certain level, I was that man, too.[35]

In this quote, Ellis discusses the unfulfilling nature of Patrick's habit of conspicuous consumption — the fact that Patrick is enslaved to a desire to live the "good life" that never really delivers true satisfaction. Ellis's comments equally apply to Brandon who has everything he wants (sex on demand) and yet nothing he needs (love and care). Brandon is a man who "has every freedom", as *Shame* film producer Iain Canning says, "and yet uses his body to create his own prison".

The iWorld offers the individual a wealth of opportunity to create themselves and live their lives as they wish. It is a great time to be alive, for in no other time have we enjoyed so much freedom to be our own person instead of having other people, or family, or religion, or culture dictate to us who we might be. Yet we see in *Shame* that the iWorld's insistence on personal freedom and self-determination can be its own form of tyranny.

The Gospel and the iWorld

Earlier I mentioned that Vanhoozer, drawing from Tillich, counsels us to discover the greatest anxiety and greatest hope of an era or culture in order to best understand it. We've considered the iPod ad, the Levi's ad, Steve Jobs' motivational rhetoric, and *The Biggest Loser* to see what stories they tell about life in the iWorld. They've taught us that the greatest hope of the iWorld is a self-actualised life where the individual is free to do what they want and become the best version of themselves they can be. We've also looked at *Up in the Air* and *Shame* and glimpsed the greatest anxiety of the iWorld: having all the freedom in the world, and yet not feeling free, or not being able to fully enjoy it. These latter texts have betrayed the recognition that the good life is not all that it is cracked up to be.

With this understanding of iWorld's greatest anxiety and greatest hope, how can the gospel speak into the iWorld? I have three suggestions for everyday theology:

1. Show how the Christian doctrine of grace relieves the iWorld pressure for the individual to change their life;

2. Show how God's call on the individual's life is far grander and more substantial than the iWorld's emphasis on self-determination;

3. Show how self-sacrifice — particularly that of Jesus — challenges the iWorld's preoccupation with unrestrained freedom.

Let's look at each of these in turn:

1. Grace not Effort

As we've seen, the iWorld regards individual fulfilment and satisfaction as a matter of personal responsibility. It emphasises the role of individual effort when it comes to improving one's lot in life. This amounts to a secular "gospel of works" — as if by working on ourselves we will attain ultimate meaning, identity and purpose.

The problem with this system is that you never know if you've "made it" unless you measure up to a standard of success offered by your peers or culture. Emma Duncan's transformation brought her into line with dominant standards of beauty and value. It's her satisfying of these standards that qualifies her as a "success". But such standards are culturally specific and subject to change — so the recognition and status they can bestow are by no means real or universally applicable.

Living up to such standards makes someone into a "horizontal self", argues Mark Sayers. The horizontal self looks to others for a sense of identity, and their peers or culture determine their understanding of what it means to live a good life. Estranged from a larger story that structures their lives and gives them meaning and purpose, horizontal selves dedicate their lives to the therapeutic ethos by endlessly working on themselves in pursuit of the earthly good life. Horizontal selves risk becoming slaves to achievement and the approval of others.[36]

However, Sayers contrasts the plight of the horizontal self with that of the "vertical self", who understands that a larger story frames their endeavours in the world. As a Christian writer, Sayers argues that the identity of the vertical self is grounded in God, rather than in the opinions of other people. God's grounding of individual identity not only provides the individual with "existential security" that reassures them of their ultimate value but also provides a context for meaningful action in every area of life. Christian vertical selves, then, are a "story-formed community"[37] whose lives and identities are shaped by the gospel — the story of God's redemption of humankind that is only possible through God's grace, rather than our human efforts to earn salvation.

The parable of the workers told in Matthew 20:1–16 is a good illustration of the gospel of grace. It tells us that essentially, all of us are eleventh-hour workers and yet enjoy a full day's wages. Its point is that God saves by grace, not by worthiness, which is radical news in an iWorld that sees us thrive or languish on the basis of our individual efforts.

2. *The Call of God*

The iWorld is obsessed with identity. Its insistence on individual freedom and self-determination offers everyone the opportunity to make something of their lives, to be self-expressed, authentic people who can live up to their potential. This is quite a romantic prospect, but one that constrains as much as it liberates. Because our identities are no longer grounded in God (the vertical self) or shaped by our culture or tradition (tWorld), we are Bauman's endlessly mobile "tourists" free to make of ourselves what we will. But the potential downside of the freedom we enjoy through our nomadic roaming and "grazing" of experience is restlessness. We remain forever unsatisfied.

An answer to this ceaseless roving is not only the Christian's identity as a vertical self, but their identity as a pilgrim. Like Bauman's tourist, the pilgrim is constantly on the move but not for the sake of movement. Rather, pilgrims always locate themselves in relation to their final destination.[38] As with the vertical self, the pilgrim understands that a cosmic story directs their movement in the world. iWorld tourists, on the other hand, only feel part of their own individual story and may struggle to find a sense of meaning and purpose beyond their individual interests.

Christian pilgrims have as their model Abraham, the first pilgrim called by God to leave his land, culture and people for a land God would show him.[39] It's striking how similar, and yet so different, is God's command in comparison to that of the iWorld. The iWorld says: depart and leave your family, tribe, tradition and religion in order to *create and fulfil yourself*. In contrast, God says that Abraham must be prepared to leave everything he knows in order to *grasp his identity and inheritance in God*: to become not just "father" but "father of many". In both cases, Abraham must depart but it is only God who knows Abraham's true identity, and only by obeying God can Abraham hope to discover it for himself.

Understanding that God has a unique call on one's life may help challenge "moral therapeutic deism" among young Christians today, for God's call for one to take up their identity in him goes far beyond the satisfaction of individual needs that constitutes the belief system. In an interview with youth pastor Kenda Creasy Dean, she says that she is "strangely hopeful" that young moral therapeutic deists can be won back by the gospel:

> The most hopeful thing for me is that young people, even though they adhere to moralistic therapeutic deism, are not giving their lives to it. It's not big enough, it doesn't matter enough, it's not substantial enough, it doesn't have enough teeth for them to give their lives to it.[40]

Dean remains positive, then, because young people aren't "giving their lives" to moral therapeutic deism as they might if it were something they really cherished. And this may be the undoing of this sham system of belief — even in an iWorld that demands no commitment to anything save the good of the individual self. For while the iWorld offers people much to live for (freedom and self-determination), it gives them no great cause for which to fight, no calling beyond the gratification of individual desire. And while a great many iWorld citizens don't mind such a state of affairs, many also intuitively sense that there is more to life than being the star of one's own story. The gospel's assertion that there is a larger narrative of which we are all a part presents a good opportunity for the gospel to flourish. A key part of that narrative concerns self-sacrifice, to which I'll now turn.

3. *Self-sacrifice*

Timothy Keller's *Counterfeit Gods* teaches us that good things — money, purpose, love and freedom — are dangerous if they become "ultimate things" on which we stake our significance, security and fulfilment. They become idols that control us "since we feel we must have them or life is meaningless".[41] Earlier, I used *Shame* to briefly explore the idea that freedom can become its own form of tyranny if pursued at all costs.

If sexual freedom is an idol, as it is in *Shame* and the iWorld at large, then most forms of sexual restraint will be rejected as prudishness. The iWorld regards limits on legal, consensual sexual behaviour as repressive, and a hangover from the tWorld that sought to control individual freedom, since the tWorld made its own idols out of traditional morality, responsibility and duty.

The general rejection of limits on behaviour doesn't just apply to sexual freedom, but for most freedoms in the iWorld. In order to ensure the liberty of the individual, we tend to operate on a "freedom from" model — we want freedom from tradition, history, convention, religion, authority, family, other people's expectations, and so on. This iWorld attitude is audible in Steve Jobs' rhetoric when he counsels people not to let others' opinions drown out their inner voice. Rather, Jobs said, people should follow their intuition and go after their dreams, for that would lead to the greatest satisfaction.

While there is wisdom in Jobs' words, they indicate the iWorld assumption that any constraint or limit is undesirable or repressive. And yet we've also seen that iWorld individuals who reject the company of others (Ryan from *Up in the Air*), satisfy their every whim (Brandon from *Shame*), or who enjoy unparalleled freedom (the average iWorld citizen), do not seem all that happy and fulfilled either. The rising rates of depression in the West testify to that.

Perhaps what we need to do is to reconfigure the way we conceive of freedom. The "freedom from" model is negative; perhaps the cure lies in the switch to a positive alternative — articulated in the terms "freedom for". Instead of asking, then, "What should we be liberated from?" we need to reframe the question to "What will we use our freedom for?"

Such a positive model of freedom ("freedom for") introduces the possibility of self-sacrifice — quite a radical idea in an iWorld dedicated to expanding the possibilities of the individual, rather than giving them up. We can see such a self-sacrificial attitude at work in a speech that J K Rowling, best-selling author of the *Harry Potter* series, gave the Harvard University graduating class of 2008.

In it, Rowling spoke of the power of imagination — which she defined as not only the ability to imagine what is not, but also the power to "empathise with humans whose experiences we have never shared".[42] Reflecting on her experience of working for Amnesty International and hearing horrible stories of people persecuted for speaking up against the brutality of their governments, she exhorted Harvard students to use their power for the good of other people:

> Your intelligence, your capacity for hard work, the education you have earned and received, give you unique status, and unique responsibilities . . . choose to use your status and influence to raise your voice on behalf of those who have no voice . . . choose to identify not only with the powerful, but with the powerless . . . choose to retain the ability to imagine yourself into the lives of those who do not have your advantages.[43]

Notice how sharply the story of the world told by Rowling's speech contrasts with Steve Jobs' commencement address. While Jobs said that it was most important to pursue your dreams, Rowling said it was most important to lift up others, to identify with the powerless. This isn't just lip service for Rowling either; it was reported in March that she's donated so much to charity that she's no longer a billionaire.[44] While Rowling still has a fortune of £646 million to her name, it's a rare sight to see rich people emptying themselves out for the sake of others.

I suspect that while most iWorld citizens would find Jobs an inspirational figure, they would find more to admire in Rowling. For Jobs exhorts people to reach for their dreams; Rowling asks that in doing so, they shouldn't forget about others but, rather, be their advocate.

If iWorld citizens can applaud Rowling's example, then marvelling at Jesus shouldn't be too hard for them either. For while Jesus had everything and was richer than the richest of billionaires, he gave it all up for the good of others (Philippians 2). Jesus lowered himself at such great cost to himself because God is other-person centred, which completely overturns the overall philosophy of the iWorld: that life is all about you. If we can make those connections between Rowling and Jesus, and show that the good we applaud in Rowling's behaviour reflects, in small part, what Jesus has done in giving his life for others, then perhaps those who admire Rowling can come to a greater admiration of Jesus. They may even come to worship him.

Some Final Thoughts

For everyday theology to be effective it must demonstrate an understanding of the preoccupations, desires and fears that drive people. As I've suggested, popular culture and everyday life are good places to start listening out for the stories our cultural texts tell about life in the brave new iWorld.

We've mostly considered the notion of individual freedom — for this is the iWorld's matter of greatest concern. As I've identified, the iWorld tends to operate on a negative model of freedom — "freedom from". In ministering to the iWorld we need, however, to restate the question in positive form through the question "what will we use our freedom for?"

I suggest that this approach is useful because it strikes a balance between the commitments of the iWorld and the tWorld. First, it insists on individual agency — which the tWorld often downplayed (at best) and suppressed (at worst) in the name of the group. And yet, in contradiction to iWorld values, this question also acknowledges that the best chance of happiness for individuals and groups is not a throwing off of all constraints but a willingness to make sacrifices for a greater good — especially the good of others.

In other words, the question "what will we use our freedom for?" indicates that our burden of selfhood in the iWorld is not simply about being free, but what to do with our freedom. The gospel gives us good reason to believe that the good life, so eagerly desired in the iWorld, is not one of self-sufficiency or unrestrained individualism, but one lived in sacrificial service to community. Jesus, above all, shows us what it means to live a good life: a willingness to use one's strengths, gifts and freedoms for the good of others.[45] And by no means does Jesus intend to hold out on us. It was he, after all, who said, "I have come that they may have life, and have it to the full" (John 10:10).

Chapter Eight

PREACHING TO THE BIRDS? THE MISSION OF THE CHURCH TO CREATION

MICK POPE

Abstract

Eco-missiology sees mission in terms of reconciliation at all levels. It recognises that the God who creates is also the God who redeems all that he has made. This holistic mission includes both eco-justice for the poor as well as care for creation for its own sake. This talk will develop an eco-missiological framework based upon a narrative reading of the Bible, including reflections on eco-praxis such as holistic mission and dialogue with environmentalists.

We're on a Mission from God

With apologies to The Blues Brothers I'd like to introduce myself. I'm on a mission from God. But also with apologies to Amos, "I am not a missiologist nor am I the son of a missiologist, for I am a meteorologist and a teacher of students" (Amos 7:14). I never intended to study missiology as a theology undergraduate. Having spent many years pondering overseas mission and deciding I was neither suited nor called to it, I decided that I didn't need missiology. However, as Frost and Hirsch have stated, the church is not truly the church unless it is missionally shaped. Like many others, I had become comfortable with Christendom, comfortable with the attractional model of church, and kind of lazy.

My journey to being an aspiring eco-missiologist is a long one, and has gone through four stages. Firstly, from a young age I developed a growing awareness of and delight in the natural world, spawned by natural curiosity, education and the right sort of television. A second important stage was a growing awareness of our impact upon the natural world, which has been ongoing with the emergence in the popular mind over the past few years of an awareness of climate change/global warming. This represents the beginning of what Pope John Paul II called an ecological conversion. Yet because humans are meant to minister rather than exercise absolute lordship over creation, ecological conversion can only occur properly after conversion to faith in the Lord Jesus. What seems to be missing in the experience of many Christians is the fourth stage: recognition of our connectedness to the rest of creation and our responsibility as God's image. This is the subject of eco-missiology and the theme of this talk.

Whose Mission? Which Mission Field?

Thus far I have assumed eco-missiology is a sensible theological concept without defining it. According to Ross Langmead, eco-missiology sees mission in terms of reconciliation at all levels. The gospel is broader than "me and Jesus" because God is involved with the whole of creation, not just human beings. Eco-missiology is concerned for creation because God saves us *with* and not *from* creation. Eco-missiology is also a matter of eco-justice, since it is the global poor who face the worst effects of environmental degradation; and includes eco-spirituality, which represents a new way of seeing creation, because it views caring for creation *in its own right* as a form of mission.

Traditional evangelical theology has had difficulty in accommodating an eco-missiology given its views of salvation. Leon Morris identifies *euangelion* as a Pauline word meaning "the news of what God has done in Christ for man's salvation". Langmead observes that many Christians hold a rather apocalyptic and dualistic view where we are saved *from* and not *with* the creation; the emphasis is on going to heaven when we die, being raptured and the earth burned up. He suggests that this is due to an overemphasis on divine transcendence and Christ's atoning work, as opposed to divine immanence and Christ as creator.

Many Christians are wary of involvement in environmental issues due to a fear of syncretism and suspicion of the "green agenda". However, the church cannot afford to ignore mission that encompasses more than the human sphere. We live in an age known as the anthropocene, where humans represent a geological force. We have become so powerful through technology that we can remove entire mountains, desolate large stretches of ocean, pollute our atmosphere, change weather patterns, and precipitate mass extinction. Sea-level rise due to global warming is already threatening some island communities such as the Carteret Islanders and the Tuvaluans. Bangladeshis are steadily losing land to sea-level rise and upstream water usage. Diseases like malaria are spreading into highland areas where previously they had been unknown. The global poor are those most sensitive to climate change; however, the developed world also seems poorly positioned to cope with the impacts as rising temperatures are likely contributing to weather extremes across the globe.

Meanwhile, we have entered into a post-Christendom phase of history in the West, one which Tom Wright describes as a pagan world much resembling the first century. The rising ecological consciousness has been accompanied by a growing interest in Eastern religions and alternate spiritualities. Since the publication of Lyn White's 1966 paper,[1] Christianity stands accused of being anthropocentric and the cause of environmental abuse in the West. While his thesis has been critiqued many times, the view remains in the popular imagination, and not without some cause. My own dialogue with some deep ecologists has typically been aggressive and dismissive of Christianity. Even in the academy, some theologians want to sideline or even ignore "grey texts" like Genesis 1:26–28.

Therefore, the missional church needs to address these concerns in its theology and praxis by rediscovering the holistic nature of the biblical narrative. In this way, we avoid falling prey to what C S Lewis called "Christianity and", the wedding of our own pet causes to the faith. Likewise, in developing a thick biblical narrative, we seek to avoid tokenism or our eco-mission being viewed as absurd as St Francis' preaching to the birds.

Once upon a Time — Mission and Eco-narrative

Worldviews, according to Wright,[2] are the pre-cognitive, pre-suppositional stages of culture that often go unexamined because they are hidden from view. Worldviews consist of four key ideas. *Narratives* or stories are the way in which we view and understand the world around us, be they religious or secular. Think, for example, of the role the story of the ANZACs plays for some Australians. From these stories we are able to address the basic questions of life such as: Who are we, why are we here? What is wrong with the world and how do we fix it? Australians, for example, often think of themselves as stoic battlers, braving the elements and hardships of life, in the ANZAC spirit. Thirdly, worldviews provide us with symbols such as events (think national holidays like ANZAC Day) and artefacts such as flags and anthems. Such symbols define communities, acting as boundary markers. Finally, praxis is the way of being in the world, the sorts of actions that a community performs, reflecting the worldview. Australian generosity is grounded in our belief of the stoic battler needing a hand from time to time to help them stand on their own two feet again. Each of these four elements interacts with and informs the other as is schematically shown below.

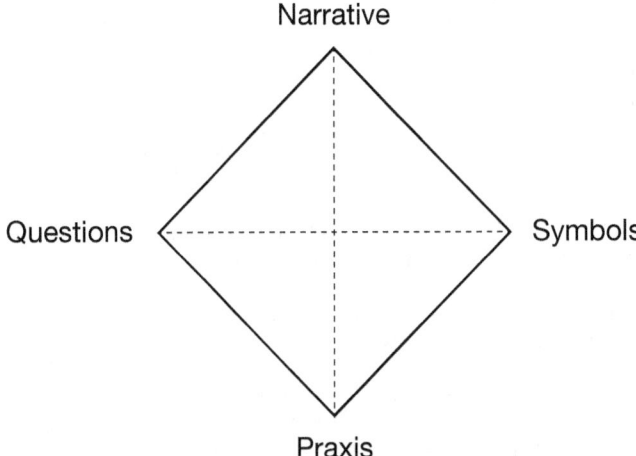

The way in which we as Christians understand issues such as the environment is critically dependent on the way we read Scripture. A US statement published by Southern Baptists declares that they could take no position on global warming since they had no special revelation. Roger Olson[3] notes that many conservative evangelicals approach Scripture as a source of propositional statements. Often they can equate their own tradition's formulation of those statements on a level close to Scripture, and form their theology as a bounded set. If there are no appropriate propositional statements for an issue, "thou shalt/shalt nots", then an issue can be ignored.

In contrast, Olson sees the Bible as a narrative. A narrative theology of Scripture is post-foundational in that it does not seek to abstract the propositions from the narrative of

Scripture to construct an indubitable, timeless set of doctrines but, instead, emphasises the transformative nature of Scripture, and recognises that such transformation does not occur solely via the transfer of information. Wright has developed a "five act" hermeneutic of Scripture as narrative, consisting of Creation, Fall, Israel, Jesus, and the Church.[4] He likens this model to a long-lost Shakespearean play where the first four acts survive intact, but only the start and the end of the fifth act are extant. What is required is an imaginative improvisation based on the available information. A careful reading of Scripture shows how each of the acts supports an eco-missiological reading. Below I trace out such a reading, with particular emphasis on the first and fifth acts.

Creation

In *The Lost World of Genesis One*,[5] John Walton recognises that Genesis 1 is ancient cosmology, with a very different ontology to the one moderns use to understand the world. Consider, for example, the difference between the ontology of a chair and that of a business. While the ontology of a chair is largely material, i.e., it involves a consideration of the materials used to make it, the design and manufacturing process, what is the ontology of a company? When does it exist? A company exists when it exists legally and begins to do business, i.e., when it is performing its function as a company. Or consider a marriage. A marriage is not physically constructed as much as legally recognised and relationally constituted. Walton argues that the best way to understand the creative acts of God in Genesis 1 is using a functional ontology.

One of the things this function/functionary model does is it ties human culture to our understanding of creation, as opposed to the reductionist perspective of science. Michael Welker notes creation is not to be simply identified with nature but includes it. This is evident, for example, in the role that lights in the sky play in marking out days, seasons and years (Gen 1:14). The heavens are the place where natural forces determine life and culture. Human beings are central to the plot, not a distraction from it. This warns us against the extremes that say large sections of the world should be set aside as "wilderness" where humans are not allowed (though the idea of reserves or world heritage areas is a valuable one) and yet as we shall see below, we need also to avoid ideas of unfettered usage.

The ordering of functions and functionaries in creation ends with God resting on the seventh day (Gen 2:2; Exod 20:11). In the Ancient Near East, temples were built so that deities could rest and exercise their divine rule. This is the subject of Psalm 132, where God's resting place is identified with the Ark and Zion, where he sits enthroned. Likewise, in Isaiah 66:1–2, heaven is God's throne and the earth his footstool. Walton concludes that Genesis 1 recounts the establishing of the function of a cosmic temple from which God can rule. Some reflection of this is found in the construction of the Jerusalem temple, with the water basin reflecting the sea and the pillars possibly pillars of the earth (1 Kgs 7). The Hebrew word for light used in connection with the tabernacle lamp (Exod 25:6) is the same used for the celestial bodies on the fourth day of creation.

So God rules from his cosmic temple, and it is here again that we see the important role given to humanity — not to serve mother earth but God himself as his representatives. Rikk Watts[6] notes there are close parallels with the account of the formation of human beings from the dust and the breathing in of the divine breath in Genesis 2, and how ancient and modern idols are made. The key to eco-mission is to recognise that creation is the temple-cosmos in which everything has a function. Our function as the *imago Dei* is to carry out the *eco-missio Dei*.

In the temple-cosmos, the non-human creation has its role in praising God. Trees in particular are given a voice (Isa 14:8, 44:23), but God is glad in all of his works (Ps 104:31) be it birds in the trees or Leviathan sporting in the sea. So long as creatures are free to do what it is they are meant to do, they fulfil their role. Psalm 104 is careful to affirm that humanity is part of, not separate from, the rest of what God has done. This Psalm therefore both affirms the value of human existence and economic activity, and the value of the rest of creation to God, and provides us with a theology of wilderness and God's care for those creatures that lie entirely outside the economic order.

Fall

The Fall (Gen 3) clearly marks a break in human-divine relationships, the repair of which is the focus of much atonement theology. Likewise chapters which follow illustrate the breakdown of human relationships in a pattern of violence and murder. Furthermore, the story of Babel illustrates the corporate nature of sin, idolatry, rebellion and the misuse of technology. What is less often emphasised is the break in relationship between humanity and the environment in the form of a curse of the ground (Gen 3:17). The culmination of this curse is the uncreation of the flood, and yet the ark represents not only the salvation of humanity but also of a selection of the non-human creation. This is a theme that Paul echoes in Romans 8, to which we will turn shortly.

Israel

The call of Abram was God's plan to undo the Fall by choosing a people for himself among whom he could dwell (Exod 29:45) and bring blessing to the whole world (Gen 12:1–3). God led his people through the exodus (Exod 13:18ff), and dwelt among them within the tabernacle above the mercy seat of the ark (Ex 25:22), which found a permanent home in the temple built during the rule of Solomon (1 Kgs 8:1ff). However, God could not be contained within creation, let alone the Jerusalem temple (1 Kgs 8:27), therefore, God's concern for all of creation is not limited by his particular relationship with a covenant people.

Land is a central theme of the Old Testament: God's people, in God's place, under God's blessing. While much of how the land is described is in terms of agricultural fertility, there are texts that treat it in a more holistic way. As well as laws covering the treatment of livestock (Deut 23:4) and their Sabbath rest (Exod 20:10), the Sabbath year (Exod 23:10–11) includes the wild animals. Furthermore, Michael Northcott notes that there is a close connection between ecological disasters and exile on one hand, and unfaithfulness to the laws and worship of Yahweh on the other in passages like Jeremiah 5:22–28. There was a direct connection between empire building and the pursuit of pagan idols of fertility, injustice and failure to keep Sabbath economics and ecology. Under such circumstances, ecological collapse was "natural" and inevitable.

Jesus

Many years ago I heard a debate at Monash University between ethicist Peter Singer and a pastor. Singer maintained that Christianity was not a useful basis for environmental ethics because Jesus cursed a fig tree to wither and die, and caused the death of a herd of swine. If we go looking for a "thou shalt plant trees" command from Jesus, we will be disappointed. Instead, we need to understand where Jesus saw himself with regards to God's unfolding narrative.

When Jesus proclaimed the gospel, what did he mean? Was it inclusive of eco-mission? *Euangelion* is found in the Greek Old Testament in passages such as Isaiah 40:9 and 52. In Isaiah 40, the heralding of the good news is proclaiming the forgiveness of sins (vv.1, 9) the coming of God (vv.3–5), and the gathering in of his flock, Israel (vv.10–11), i.e., the return from exile. Israel's exile was the result of breaking the covenant with Israel's God (Deut 28:63–68) by committing idolatry. Isaiah therefore reaffirms the superiority of the God of Israel over pagan idols (v12ff, especially vv18–20). Wright[7] suggests that

> many first-century Jews thought of themselves as living in a continuing narrative stretching from earliest times, through ancient prophesies, and on towards a climactic moment of deliverance which might come at any moment,

and that "this continuing narrative was currently seen, on the basis of Daniel 9, as a long passage through a state of continuing 'exile'". Be it Roman or Persian, if Gentiles were in charge, God was not truly king.

Hence, *euangelion* carried with it a world of meaning: God's forgiveness, end of exile and political oppression, and the blessing of Israel's God. Paul's contention is that the salvific promises made to Israel are fulfilled in the gospel of Jesus. To suggest that Jesus (Mark 1:14–15) or Paul (Rom 1) somehow "spiritualise" the word *euangelion*, emptying it of all political meaning, beggars belief. The contemporary secular usage is illuminating:

> a saviour for us and those who come after us, to make war to cease, to create order everywhere . . .; the birthday of the god [Augustus] was the beginning for the world of the *glad tidings* that have come to men through him . . . (emphasis added)[7]

The value of this broader view of the gospel for eco-mission is firstly that people are not saved from the earth but expect to be renewed with the earth: God's people in God's place. Any well-thought-out resurrection theology should also make this clear. Secondly, the gospel challenges all empires, and empires tend to be inherently destructive of the environment, be they Rome or profit-driven, multinational, petroleum companies.

Related to this understanding of the gospel and the kingdom of God is the model of the atonement know as *Christus Victor*. As N T Wright notes in his *Evil and the Justice of God*,[8] this is the view that, on the cross, Jesus has won a victory over the powers of evil. The view of evil presented is non-dualistic in that it recognises with Solzhenitsyn that:[9]

> If only there were evil people somewhere insidiously committing evil deeds, and it were necessary only to separate them from the rest of us and destroy them. But the line dividing good and evil cuts through the heart of every human being.

Further, evil is not simply individual but can be corporate and systemic. The path that led to the cross was a downward spiral of evil, from the ever-present Roman empire as discussed above, to the corruption of Israel and her temple, and the shadowy, supra-personal powers of darkness lurking in the background. These powers of darkness could enter into Judas, or be personified in attitudes like Peter's to Jesus' vocation. In dealing with evil, Jesus identified with Israel, warned her of the consequences of her actions and stood in her place, and in the place of all of humanity on the cross. Wright is worth quoting at length here:

> Jesus suffers the full consequences of evil, evil from the political, social, cultural, personal, moral, religious and spiritual angles all rolled into one, evil in the downward spiral hurtling towards the pit of destruction and despair. And he does so precisely as the act of redemption, of taking that downward fall and exhausting it, so that there may be new creation, new covenant, forgiveness, freedom and hope . . . The call of the gospel is for the church to *implement* the victory of God in the world *through suffering love*.[10]

It is this view of the cross that makes it easier to affirm with Paul that Christ reconciles *all things* to himself (Col 1:20; Eph 1:10) through that suffering love, and waits, we shall see below, for us to suffer with creation for its redemption.

The Church

The age of the church is the age of the Spirit, the age between the coming of Christ and his return. Sadly there is much misunderstanding about the nature of this return and hence the mission of the church. Perhaps the clearest passage with implications for eco-mission is Romans 8:19–23. In Romans, Paul explains how God is true to his covenant promises in the face of Jewish unbelief. God achieves this through the Messiah Jesus, who is God come in the flesh. Those who are in the Messiah are "sons of God" (Rom 8:14) just as Israel was (Exod 4:23), led by the indwelling Spirit (Rom 8:9–11) as Israel was by the fiery pillar, having been rescued from slavery to sin just as Israel had been rescued from slavery in Egypt. The parallel with the exodus is even more striking if we allow the identification of baptism (Rom 6) as passing through the waters of the Sea of Reeds (1 Cor 10:2). Therefore, just as Israel was led into the Promised Land, so Romans 8 does not end with eternity in heaven, but the future of the whole earth.

The personification of creation together with its co-groaning with humanity, and its eventual liberation, all bestow upon it dignity without reducing to pantheism. This groaning is no mere metaphor but based upon Paul's observations. Rome was responsible for significant deforestation as the result of timber harvesting for construction and metal smelting. This led to an increase in malarial infections, as well as flooding, river mouth silting, and soil erosion in the vicinity of Rome. Erosion was widespread in ancient Rome and Greece, as well as microclimate change, leading to a decline in agricultural production. Such are the results of empire, in stark contrast to Horace's claim that "Caesar has brought back fertile crops to the fields". This should remind us of the negative consequences of the modern agricultural revolution, including eutrophication of waterways due to overuse of fertilisers, the affects of pesticides on bees, salinity, desertification, etc.

The futures of the creation and of the children of God are intertwined. The creation longs for the future revealing of the sons of God (Rom 8:19) and groans in birth pains while we groan for our sonship (v 23), because when we are revealed as the children of God, the creation will find its own liberation (v 21). Just as humanity was given over to sin (Rom 1:18–32) and now in Christ through the Spirit hopes for resurrection (8:23–24), so the creation was subject to futility in hope (v 20). We have the first fruits of the Spirit as those who will be raised by the one who raised Christ. The creation co-groans with the sons of God, for as the first fruits we prefigure a greater harvest which includes all things. There are hints of the pneumatological groaning as well. The Spirit groans for us in our weakness as we groan for redemption, and the creation groans for its redemption too, tied up with ours. It seems then that there is a sense in which the Spirit that hovered over the waters of creation (Gen 1:2) even now groans with it.

Because only the God who subjected creation to frustration can liberate it from that frustration, what does this say for our eco-missiological task? Firstly, we should groan with creation, empathetically feeling its suffering and the suffering that others experience as a result of our misrule. This includes a sense of mourning and of contrition. Secondly, we are called to live in hope; hope that God will return and put everything to rights, including the state of the creation. This hope energises action instead of leading to apathy. Likewise, while we are to feel appropriate guilt, we are not to be paralysed by it nor motivated solely by it. Hope is our watchword, as we live proleptically in the light of the redemption that creation will share with us. And this hope informs our sense of justice as we see human and natural ecology out of shape, and work to alleviate the suffering of others who suffer because of environmental degradation. As one day God's shalom will extend to all things, we should seek peacemaking with each other and with the creation now.

Reframing Our Symbols and Questions

We can see from the preceding discussion that we can re-frame some of the classic questions of Christian theology in light of this more holistic view of mission.

Who are we? We are created in the image of God to bear this image to the rest of creation, ruling over it and caring for it as his servants in his temple-cosmos. Human flourishing relies upon maintaining good relationships with God and with each other and carrying out our responsibilities to care for creation. The bestowal of the *imago Dei* implies the carrying out of the *eco-missio Dei*.

What's the problem? The Fall represents broken relationships with God, each other and the creation, leading to its groaning under our misrule as we either treat it as divine or disposable. As a result, human and natural ecologies are warped out of shape.

What's the solution? The cross, where Jesus defeats evil in all of its forms and reconciles all things to himself.

What time is it? We live not in some Edenic past, nor some heavenly future, but in the age of the Spirit where all creation groans, awaiting Christ's return and the revealing of the children of God. Until that occurs, individual and corporate greed and idolatry lead to human and non-human suffering.

What are we to do? The great Commission calls us to make disciples of all nations so that the people of God may be formed out of every nation, tribe and tongue. This discipleship includes not only instruction of right belief and practice in personal virtues, but peace, justice and wise rule over creation. We live proleptically in light of a future where the whole creation finally attains to its divine telos.

There are also a number of symbols or boundary markers of the Christian life that need to be understood in a broader context. Two that Wright refers to are baptism and the Eucharist or Lord's Supper. In the case of the former, water is a symbol of the inner cleansing of the Spirit, an outward visible sign of an inward invisible grace as Anglicans would say. Scripture attests not only to the purifying but life-giving nature of water (e.g. John 4). As the universal solvent for life, and a potentially future scarce resource with changing rainfall regimes and contamination, God's people should value water more and employ its symbolism in more imaginative ways. Christians should affirm, if somewhat tentatively, Loren Eiseley who said "If there is magic on the planet, it is contained in Water".

The Eucharist or Lord's Supper is often a performance and a fast-food version of kingdom table fellowship. The reality that we are the children of God awaiting our adoption is expressed in the celebration of a corporate meal that remembers that this adoption was purchased at great price. As God's new body politic on earth, we corporately practise all that the new creation will entail: peace, justice and harmony with the created order. This harmony will entail just eating, the proper consideration of the impact of our diet on the environment, and the justice or otherwise of the economics of the food consumed. Missiologically both to creation and our multicultural neighbours this may include halal and vegetarian or vegan meals. It should almost certainly include home-grown produce, attempting to heal the rift between garden and table that urbans often experience. Perhaps too, associations of harvest festival with Pentecost could be more strongly drawn, especially in less liturgically based communities.

Finally, prayer and worship, as defining features of any Christian community, should go a lot further in recognising the role the creation plays doxologically. Likewise, in lament, confession and petition, creation should receive due attention, and I draw attention to Hope for Creation, a day of prayer on climate change which will happen in September of this year (http://hopeforcreation.com.au/).

Eco-praxis

Eco-praxis is eco-missiology in practice; action informed and shaped by the holistic narrative described above, dealing with the questions it raises and the symbols that define an eco-missiologically oriented community. So what sorts of things might this involve?

Dialogue

The sharing of the gospel is to be incarnational and contextual. Although the present environmental crisis requires us to rediscover the "deep green ecology" of Scripture, there has always been a green subculture that requires us to be incarnational in our mission, i.e., the credibility of our witness comes not from the strength of our convictions or the thickness of our narrative alone, but from the dirt under our fingernails. That being said, the thickness of our narrative will ensure we can dialogue with and work alongside those with whom we share common concerns but who live under different narratives.

One the one hand, we need to recognise the warnings of Romans 1 and the dangers of idolatry. Creation will not be saved either by seeing it as divine as some eco-pagans do, or as disposable as the dualistic end of Christianity does. To engage in eco-mission will mean taking flak from both sides. To one reader of my blog, ethos-environment.blogspot.com, I am pagan for suggesting Christians should recognise Earth Hour. To an environmentalist blogger, I am supposed to keep my religion out of the discussion of environmental issues. The church and its adherents have done too little, too late and stand condemned of ecocide! At various times and places this charge may stick. Tim Flannery once recounted how the efforts of Baptist missionaries in PNG to end pagan beliefs in a sacred grove led to a decline in bird of paradise numbers in an area. The narrative I have offered could both demythologise nature but still recognise it as God's sacred cosmos-temple filled with creatures valuable to him. The narrative that led to the grove's destruction is anaemic compared to this vision.

Therefore, while we recognise the uniqueness of the gospel and the dangers of idolatry, we need to seek fruitful dialogue, and Acts 17 provides a useful model. In seeking a close connection with nature, some environmentalists are following their God-given inclinations to seek him out. What is required is to show that Jesus is the creator of all they value, and that he too values it and died so that we might be reconciled to the triune God, and as a result with each other and the creation. We should be slow to speak and quick to listen to critiques of the church's role in past creation abuse. Likewise, there may be much that we can learn from others in how to value nature.

Gardening provides an opportunity to connect gospel, community and creation together in a holistic fashion. In an excellent paper presented at the Australian Association of Mission Studies Conference in 2011, Miriam Pepper provided a number of examples where Australian churches have become involved with local communities. The traditional model of mission has been attractional, where seekers are invited into our space on a Sunday morning or evening. The rest of the week, church facilities are largely unused. A church garden that invites community involvement provides a shared space that is both attractional and incarnational. It is a space of dialogue, of shared interest and activity. Church-run community gardens are not merely a front door into the real business of church; they are church. These gardens are gospel-centred communities where the biblical narrative is re-enacted, and where reconciliation is modelled on all levels. They provide the opportunities to form relationships and share the gospel through conversations while tilling the soil. Yet such shared tasks of Earth care, organic food growing and reconciliation with the soil are sharing the gospel message in all its fullness. The connections that can then be drawn via fetes and festivals such as harvest festivals and the broader community close the gap between "Sunday and Monday".

As Pepper notes, garden-based eco-missiology is deeply contextual; there is no one-size-fits-all. In some settings, community gardens provide opportunities for local migrants to connect with each other and others in their community, providing language and social skills. In others, food produced is provided for those living with HIV/AIDS. In others still, gardens provide community hubs for artists, schools, musicians and Indigenous Australians.

A final example is the work of A Rocha (www.arocha.org). A Rocha describes themselves as "an international Christian organization which, inspired by God's love, engages in scientific research, environmental education and community-based conservation projects". A Rocha's name comes from the Portuguese for "the Rock", named after their first initiative begun in 1983, which was a field study centre in Portugal in an important wetland. They are now in over 19 countries, with a small group of us trying to establish it in Australia as well. A Rocha bases their work on five Cs. The first is Christian, stating that "Underlying all we do is our biblical faith in the living God, who made the world, loves it and entrusts it to the care of human society". Theologically, A Rocha is broadly evangelical. Secondly, A Rocha is focussed on conservation: "We carry out research for the conservation and restoration of the natural world and run environmental education programmes for people of all ages". Thirdly, A Rocha focuses on community, and many of their projects involve Christians living locally in community near or within the habitat they are caring for. Fourthly, A Rocha is cross-cultural, committed to drawing "on the insights and skills of people from diverse cultures, both locally and around the world". It is a sincere hope of those of us involved in starting A Rocha in Australia that at least some of our projects will involve Indigenous Australians and learn from their long history of living in harmony with the land. Finally, A Rocha believes in cooperation "with a wide variety of organisations and individuals who share our concerns for a sustainable world". One can see in this the need for a strong narrative to sustain action and to work with others with clarity and integrity with our Christian beliefs.

Following on from these five Cs, A Rocha projects are deeply contextual. In Kenya, forests are protected and mangroves planted, and communities educated to protect their natural resources. Eco-tourism is developed and money used to provide bursaries for local students to pursue a secondary school education. Hence, unlike the caricature of environmental work, environment is not put before people, but the two are wedded together. In Lebanon, a wetland — also an important bird habitat — was protected. In addition, the visitor's centre provided an important opportunity for reconciliation between Muslim and Christian communities. In the UK, an urban space that was used for dumping rubbish was found to be a habitat for some unique plant and insect species. The land now represents an important shared space for wildlife and school and community groups in the middle of London. As has been highlighted in a number of recent books, our understanding of what represents wilderness, our proximity to it and our willingness to work with it, needs to be rethought.

Questions and Challenges

Hopefully I have been able to demonstrate that the concept of eco-mission runs deeply through the biblical narrative and is more substantial than greenwashing the gospel in the name of relevancy, and more lucid than "preaching to the birds". Eco-mission leaves us with questions and challenges for mission in theory and in praxis. Given the environmental challenges we face in the twenty-first century and the crisis of narrative that modernism in its faith in progress has produced, and then the confusion and return to paganism that postmodernism has followed, how will we respond? How can we revision our theology, from our understanding of the Godhead to the nature of the atonement to address these issues, to be the church incarnate in the world and yet be true to the biblical narrative. Indeed, how do we resist the ever-present challenge that paganism presents? We will be critiqued strongly from within our own ranks as addressing Yahweh as my Baal (Hosea 2:16) and from without as being hopelessly part of the problem.

The challenges to praxis will be to learn how to leave the four walls of our churches to embrace soil and community. Will we be willing to move church services from inside the buildings to Clean Up Australia activities, to invite others into our open spaces to till and toil, giving up some of our autonomy to the wishes of others? Are we willing to chain ourselves to trains or trees in the service of the gospel, to take up the plight of the bleating and mooing who suffer? Just as Christ surrendered his hands to nails, will we surrender ours to the soil in order to bring healing? Will we groan with creation until he returns?

CONTRIBUTORS

MICHAEL DUNCAN

Having pastored churches in Dunedin, Melbourne and Auckland, and having directed Servants to Asia's Urban Poor in the Philippines while living in the slums of Manila, Michael Duncan is now the director of Alongsiders, a youth support service in New Zealand. He has degrees in sociology and theology, and has authored several books including *Wild Ones* (UNOH Publications, Dandenong, 2006). He travels and speaks extensively in Australia and New Zealand inviting people to be there for those who stand alone.

MARY FISHER

Since 2005, Mary Fisher has been the pastor of the international congregation of the Sydney Chinese Alliance Church in Rockdale in Sydney's south. Prior to taking up that appointment, Mary spent 28 years overseas as a missionary, missions director and theology lecturer, most notably as Lecturer in Biblical Theology and Systematics at Asbury Seminary in Kentucky. She has also had a long association in the USA with IVP and the Urbana conference.

MICHAEL FROST

Dr Michael Frost is the founding Director of the Tinsley Institute, a mission study centre located at Morling College in Sydney, Australia. He is the author or editor of thirteen theological books, the most notable of which are *The Shaping of Things to Come* (2003), *Exiles* (2006) and *The Road to Missional* (2012). He was one of the founders of the Forge Mission Training Network and the founder of the missional Christian community, smallboatbigsea, based in Manly in Sydney's north. He travels and speaks extensively around the world.

SIMON CAREY HOLT

Dr Simon Carey Holt is Lecturer in Practical Theology and Associate Dean for Graduate Studies at Whitley College, Melbourne. With a background in church planting and pastoral leadership, Simon completed postgraduate studies at Fuller Seminary in California, before teaching spirituality, ethics and pastoral theology at Macquarie Christian Studies Institute at Macquarie University. He is the author of *God Next Door* (Acorn Press, Melbourne, 2007).

DARRELL JACKSON

Dr Darrell Jackson has been Senior Lecturer in Missiology at Morling since 2012. A Baptist pastor, he has worked for the Baptist Union of Great Britain, the Conference of European Churches, and most recently founded and directed the Nova Research Centre at Redcliffe College in the UK. He has written extensively in the areas of European mission and intercultural Christianity, Orthodox mission, migration and diaspora missiology. He serves the Lausanne Movement and the WEA Mission Commission in a variety of ways.

JON OWEN

Jon Owen has been a community worker with Urban Neighbours of Hope, a missionary order among the poor, since 1997. He launched the Sydney chapter of UNOH among the urban poor of Mt Druitt where he lives with his wife and daughters in one of Australia's largest and most notorious public housing estates. He is the author of *Muddy Spirituality* (UNOH Publishing, Dandenong, 2011).

MICK POPE

Melbourne-based, Mick Pope has a PhD in meteorology from Monash University and is currently enrolled in a Master of Theology. Mick is the coordinator of an environmental think-tank for Ethos: EA Centre for Christianity and Society; he also advises TEAR on climate change and eco-theology and is a Fellow of ISCAST, the Institute for the Study of Christianity in an Age of Science and Technology.

JUSTINE TOH

Dr Justine Toh is Senior Research Fellow at the Centre for Public Christianity in Sydney. She is also an Honorary Associate in the Department of Media, Music and Cultural Studies at Macquarie University. Justine is widely published in journals of media studies and business and is a regular contributor to the ABC religion website.

STUART MURRAY WILLIAMS

Dr Stuart Murray Williams spent 12 years as an urban church planter in East London and has continued to be involved in church planting as a trainer, mentor, writer, strategist and consultant. He was Oasis Director of Church Planting and Evangelism at Spurgeon's College, London. Under the auspices of the Anabaptist Network, he works as a trainer and consultant, with particular interest in urban mission, church planting and emerging forms of church. He is the founder of Urban Expression. He has written extensively on church planting, urban mission, emerging church, the challenge of post-Christendom and the Anabaptist tradition.

ENDNOTES

Chapter One
THE PRACTICE OF PLACED MISSION

1. Jane Jacobs, *The Death and Life of Great American Cities (Penguin, 1994; orig. 1961) p.14.*
2. God in Creation p.47.
3. T J Gorringe, *A Theology of the Built Environment: Justice, Power, Redemption (Cambridge: Cambridge University Press) 2002, pp185–192.*
4. Gorringe, p.185–186.
5. M Smith, J Whiteleg and N Williams, *Greening the Built Environment (London: Earthscan, 1998) p.173.*
6. Ibid. p.188.
7. Ibid.
8. Sermon for the Southwark Diocese Centenary, July 2005, in *Faith in the Cities para 5.42*
9. Ibid. p.190.
10. Ibid.
11. http://www.sydneyalliance.org.au/
12. Ibid.
13. Ibid. p.92.
14. *Faith in the Cities, para 2.68*
15. Nona Willis Aronowitz, "Most Americans Want a Walkable Neighborhood, Not a Bike House", Good, http://www.good.is/post/most-americans-want-a-walkable-neighborhood-not-a-big-house
16. Metrospiritual (56).
17. Kathleen Norris, *The Cloister Walk (London: Penguin Books, 1996) p.244.*
18. Charles Taylor, *A Secular Age (Cambridge, Mass.: Harvard University Press, 2007) p.26.*
19. Wendell Berry, "The Futility of Global Thinking", *Harpers, September 16, 1989, p.22.*
20. Alan Roxburgh, "Practices of Christian Life — Forming and Performing a Culture" in *The Journal of Missional Practice,* http://themissionalnetwork.com/index.php/practices-of-christian-life-forming-and-performing-a-culture
21. Ibid.
22. *Shaping 1st ed. p.65.*
23. Wendell Berry, "On Work", *The Art of the Commonplace, Counterpoint, 2002.*

Chapter Two
MISSION AFTER CHRISTENDOM

1. Steve Bruce, *God is Dead: Secularization in the West (Oxford: Blackwell, 2002).*
2. For example, Grace Davie, *Religion in Britain since 1945: Believing without Belonging (Oxford: Blackwell, 1994);* Rodney Stark and William Bainbridge, *A Theory of Religion (New York: Peter Lang, 1987).*
3. Acts 10.
4. Steve Chalke and Alan Mann, *The Lost Message of Jesus* (Grand Rapids: Zondervan, 2003). Several other evangelicals had previously expressed the same conviction, but none in such a popular paperback and none with Steve Chalke's profile and influence.
5. The material in this section is adapted from Stuart Murray: *Church after Christendom* (Milton Keynes: Paternoster, 2006) chapter 5.
6. Matthew 5:13–16.
7. Andrew Walls, *The Cross-Cultural Process in Christian History (Edinburgh: T&T Clark, 2002).*
8. Michael Frost, *Exiles: Living Missionally in a Post-Christian Culture* (Peabody: Hendrickson, 2006).
9. Stanley Hauerwas and William Willimon, *Resident Aliens (Nashville: Abingdon, 1991).*

Chapter Three
FITTING INTO THE TRIUNE GOD'S MISSIONAL PLOT

[1] Herbert Butterfield, *The Origins of Modern Science, p.110*

Chapter Four
FOLLOWING JESUS INTO SUBURBIA

[1] Graeme Davison, Tony Dingle, and Seamus O'Hanlon, eds. *The Cream Brick Frontier: Histories of Australian Suburbia*, Monash Publications in History No. 19 (Clayton: Department of History, Monash University, 1995).

[2] This was a claim first made by William Schneider for the United States of America in "Rule Suburbia: America in the 90s." *National Journal* 39, (1991): pp. 2335–36. However, it was true of Australia long before it was true of the USA. See Donald Horne, *The Lucky Country* (Ringwood: Penguin, 1964), who back in the 1960s claimed Australia as 'the first suburban nation'.

[3] Tony Dingle, "People and Places in Post-War Melbourne". In *The Cream Brick Frontier: Histories of Australian Suburbia*, edited by Graeme Davison, Tony Dingle and Seamus O'Hanlon, 27–40. (Clayton: Department of History, Monash University, 1995), p.30.

[4] Albert Y. Hsu, *The Suburban Christian: Finding Spiritual Vitality in the Land of Plenty* (Downers Grove: IVP Books, 2006), p.183.

[5] David Goodman, "Comparative Urban and Suburban History: An Interview with Kenneth Jackson." *Australasian Journal of American Studies* 12, no. 1 (1993), p.65.

[6] Allan Ashbolt, "Godzone: Myth and Reality." *Meanjin* 25, no. 107 (1966), p.373.

[7] Tim Rowse, "Heaven and a Hills Hoist: Australian Critics on Suburbia." *Meanjin* 37, no. 1 (1978): pp.3–13; Alan Gilbert, "The Roots of Anti-Suburbanism in Australia." In *Australian Cultural History*, edited by S.L. Goldberg and F.B. Smith, pp.33–49 (Cambridge: Cambridge University Press, 1988); Brett W. Hawkins and Stephen L. Percy, "On Anti-Suburban Orthodoxy." *Social Science Quarterly* 72, no. 3 (1991): pp.478–90.

[8] James Button, "The Suburbs: A Dream or Nightmare?" *The Age*, August 21 2004, Insight 4.

[9] Quoted by Janet Hawley, "Be It Ever So Humungous".*Good Weekend: The Age Magazine*, August 23 2003, p.25.

[10] Hawley, p.25.

[11] Andrew Hamilton, "Theology and the Suburbs". In *Developing an Australian Theology*, edited by Peter Malone, pp.87–104 (Strathfield: St Pauls Publications, 1999).

[12] Hamilton, p.88.

[13] Eric O Jacobsen, *Sidewalks in the Kingdom: New Urbanism and the Christian Faith*. Edited by David S Cunningham and William T Cavanaugh, The Christian Practice of Everyday Life (Grand Rapids: Brazos Press, 2003), p.14.

[14] Jacobsen, p.15.

[15] David L Goetz, *Death by Suburb: How to Keep the Suburbs from Killing Your Soul* (New York: HarperCollins, 2006).

[16] Mike Erre, *The Jesus of Suburbia: How We Tamed the Son of God to Fit Our Lifestyle* (Nashville: Thomas Nelson, 2006).

[17] Erre, p.3.

[18] Joel S Hirschhorn, *Sprawl Kills: How Blandburbs Steal Your Time, Health and Money* (Sterling & Ross, 2005); Robert M Fogelson, *Bourgeois: Suburbia, 1870–1930* (Yale University Press, 2005).

[19] For example, see Marion Halligan, *The Taste of Memory* (Crows Nest: Allen &Unwin, 2004), p.15.

[20] Linda Mercadante, "Tasting the Bitter with the Sweet: The Spiritual Geography of Newark, New Jersey". In *Spirit in the Cities: Searching for Soul in the Urban Landscape*, edited by Kathryn Tanner, pp.47–68 (Minneapolis: Fortress Press, 2004). See also Kathleen Norris, *Dakota: A Spiritual Geography* (New York: Houghton Mifflin, 1993).

[21] Ezro F P Luttmer, "Neighbors as Negatives: Relative Earnings and Well-Being". In *Faculty Research Working Paper Series* (Cambridge MA: J.F. Kennedy School of Government, Harvard University, 2004).

[22] Lewis Mumford, *The Culture of Cities* (London: Secker and Warburg, 1938), p.215.

[23] Michael Winkler, "The Grass Is Riz". *The Age*, September 1 2004, A3 pp.4–5.

[24] Simon Carey Holt, *God Next Door: Spirituality and Mission in the Neighbourhood* (Brunswick East: Acorn Press, 2007), chapter 2.

[25] Jill Stark, "Safety Concerns Leave Australians out of Step".*The Age*, October 24 2006, p.6.

[26] Quoted by Stark, p.6.

ENDNOTES

27 Helen Brownlee and Peter McDonald, "A Safe Place for Children: Views from the Outer Suburbs". *Family Matters* 33, (December 1992): pp.22–26.

28 Quoted by Joff Smith, "Loath Thy Neighbour". *The Sunday Age*, March 28 1993, Agenda 3. Smith refers to the research undertaken by Lyn Richards and published as *Nobody's Home: Dreams and Realities in a New Suburb* (Melbourne: Oxford University Press, 1990).

29 Setha M. Low, *Behind the Gates: Life, Security, and the Pursuit of Happiness in Fortress America* (New York: Routledge, 2003).

30 Jane Cadzow, "Do Fence Me In". *The Age Good Weekend*, May 5 2007, pp.33–40.

31 Graeme Davison, *The Past and Future of the Australian Suburb*. Edited by Rita C. Coles, Urban Research Program Working Papers (Canberra: Australian National University, 1993), pp.3–5.

32 Brendan Gleeson, *Australian Heartlands: Making Space for Hope in the Suburbs* (Crows Nest: Allen & Unwin, 2006), p.73.

33 From Peterson's forward to Jacobsen, *Sidewalks in the Kingdom, p.9*.

34 Quoted by Leslie Griffiths, "Living in Knowable Communities". In *Spirituality in the City*, edited by Andrew Walker, 43–54 (London: SPCK, 2005), p.49.

35 John Brinckerhoff Jackson, *A Sense of Place, a Sense of Time* (Newhaven: Yale University Press, 1994).

36 David Matzko McCarthy, *The Good Life: Genuine Christianity for the Middle Class*. Edited by David S. Cunningham and William T. Cavanaugh, *The Christian Practice of Everyday Life* (Grand Rapids: Brazos Press, 2004).

37 McCarthy, p.94.

38 McCarthy, p.118.

39 Rowan Williams, "Urbanization, the Christian Church and the Human Project". In *Spirituality in the City*, edited by Andrew Walker, pp.15–26 (London: SPCK, 2005), p.17.

40 Quoted by Williams, p.24.

41 Anne Buttimer, "Home, Reach, and the Sense of Place". In *The Human Experience of Space and Place*, edited by Anne Buttimer and David Seamon, pp.166–87 (New York: St. Martin's Press, 1980).

42 Fiona Allon, *Renovation Nation: Our Obsession with Home* (Sydney: University of New South Wales Press, 2008).

43 Allon, chapter 2.

44 Allon, p.41.

45 Allon, p.205.

46 Allon, p.205.

47 Hsu, *The Suburban Christian*, p.53.

Chapter Five
LOST IN SALVATION

1 Romans 14:10–12, 2 Corinthians 5:10, 1 Corinthians 3, Romans 2:1–16.

2 According to the *Oxford Concise Dictionary of the Christian Church, ecclesiology concerns itself with two dimensions: (1) the science of the building and decoration of the Churches; (2) the theology of the Church, p. 188.*

3 http://jmm.aaa.net.au/articles/8576.htm

4 George Barna, *Revolution (Tyndale, 2005), p. 49.*

5 Tony and Felicity Dale/George Barna, *The Rabbit and the Elephant (Tyndale, 2009), p. xii.*

6 Ed Stetzer, "Understanding the Emerging Church," *Baptist Press, January 6, 2006* www.sbcbaptistpress.org/bpnews.asp?ID=22406

7 Jim Belcher, *Deep Church: A Third Way Beyond Emerging and Traditional (Downers Grove, Illinois; IVP Books, 2009), p.46.*

8 Ed Stetzer, p.2.

9 Jim Belcher, p.46.

10 Ibid., p.47.

11 William J Abraham, *The Logic of Evangelism (Grand Rapids, Michigan: William B. Eerdmans Publishing Company, 1989), p.101.*

12 Ibid., p.19.

13 Ibid., p.34.

14 Ibid., p.108.

15. E Stanley Jones, *Conversion* (London, UK: Abingdon Press, 1960), p. 26.
16. George Gallup, Jr., and George O'Connell, *Who Do Americans Say That I Am?* (Philadelphia: Westminster, 1986), pp.88–89.
17. Ronald J Sider, *The Scandal of the Evangelical Conscience* (Grand Rapids, Michigan: BakerBooks, 2005), pp.12–13.
18. William J Abraham, p.113.
19. See, S. B. Ferguson, 'Ordo Salutis' in *New Dictionary of Theology* (Leicester, England: Inter-Varsity Press, 1988), pp.480–1.
20. N T Wright, "New Perspectives on Paul" in *Justification in Perspective* edited by Bruce McCormack (Grand Rapids, Michigan: Baker & Rutherford House, 2006).
21. Randy Maddox, Responsible Grace: John Wesley's Practical Theology (Nashville, Tennessee: Kingswood Books, 1994).
22. Reconstructed from Wright's "New Perspectives on Paul" in Justification in Perspective edited by Bruce McCormack (2006). Paul Helm in his analysis of Wright's ordo salutis, has it this way:

Divine foreknowledge
Divine 'marking out ahead of time'
Calling
Justification/Vindication
Sanctification
Glorification

Paul Helm "Analysis 4 — Bishop N.T. Wright's ordo *salutis*" in *Helm's Deep: Philosophical Theology, Monday, July 02, 2007:* http://paulhelmsdeep.blogspot.com/2007/07/analysis-4-

23. Sermon 9, "The Spirit of Bondage and of Adoption" *Works, 1:251. Wesley writes: For his soul is in a deep sleep: His spiritual senses are not awake; they discern neither spiritual good nor evil. The eyes of his understanding are closed; they are sealed together, and see not. Clouds and darkness continually rest upon them; for he lies in the valley of the shadow of death. Hence having no inlets for the knowledge of spiritual things, all the avenues of his soul being shut up, he is in gross, stupid ignorance of whatever he is most concerned to know. He is utterly ignorant of God, knowing nothing concerning him as he ought to know. He is totally a stranger to the law of God, as to its true, inward, spiritual meaning. He has no conception of that evangelical holiness, without which no man shall see the Lord; nor of the happiness which they only find whose life is hid with Christ in God.*
24. Sermon 9, *Works 1:251–254.*
25. Robert Wuthnow, *Creative Spirituality: The Way of the Artist* (California, US: California University Press, 2003).
26. Lynne and Bill Hybels, *Rediscovering Church: The Story & Vision of Willow Creek Community Church* (Grand Rapids, Michigan: Zondervan Publishing House, 1995).
27. Luke 15:11–32.
28. Kenneth Bailey, specialist in Middle Eastern New Testament Studies, argues that from the Parable of the Prodigal Son one cannot use the phrase "He came to himself" as a point of repentance. Bailey writes, "However, this view overlooks a critical aspect of the chapter as a whole. As noted, in the parable of the lost sheep, Jesus redefines repentance as 'acceptance of being found.' Neither the lost sheep nor the lost coin find themselves. Rather, the shepherd and the woman, at great cost in time and effort, find their lost sheep and coin. Repentance is thus something done for the believer. It is not something the believer does for himself/herself." [Kenneth E. Bailey, *Finding the Lost: Cultural Keys to Luke 15 (St. Louis, US: Concordia Publishing House, 1992), pp.129–130*].
29. Luke 3: 7–14.
30. Matthew 25:31–46.
31. Randy L. Maddox, *Responsible Grace: John Wesley's Practical Theology* (Nashville, Tennessee: Kingswood Books, 1994), pp.157–8.
32. Scot McKnight posits that iGens, those aged between 18–30 (2010), are by and large those who will not respond initially to any message declaring that they are sinners. This age group, however, does like Jesus, so McKnight urges that we start with the Gospels in our conversations with iGens. They warm to Jesus because of his fight against injustice and systemic evil. In time, presses McKnight, the iGen "will realize that systemic sin is linked to personal sin. Suddenly he or she feels accountable to God." See "The Gospel for iGens" by Scot McKnight in *ChristianityToday.Com:* www.christinaitytoday.com/le/communitylife/evangelism/thegospelforigens.html
33. Tom Wright, *Justification: God's Plan and Paul's Vision* (London, UK: SPCK, 2009), p.7.
34. See John Piper's *The Future of Justification: A Response to N.T. Wright* (Wheaton, IL: Crossway Books, 2007) and Tom Wright's response to Piper in his *Justification: God's Plan and Paul's Vision* (London, UK: SPCK, 2009).
35. Paul G. Hiebert, "The Category 'Christian' in the Mission Task," in *International Review of Missions* 72 (1983), pp.421–27.
36. Michael Frost and Alan Hirsch, *The Shape of Things to Come: Innovation and Mission for the 21st Century Church* (Peabody, Massachusetts:

ENDNOTES

Hendrickson Publishers, 2003), p.47.

[37] William J Abraham, p.100.

[38] Paul G. Hiebert, *Transforming Worldviews: An Anthropological Understanding of How People Change (Grand Rapids, Michigan: BakerAcademic, 2008), p.309.*

[39] Ibid. pp.309–310.

[40] Ibid., p.311.

[41] William J Abraham, p.107.

Chapter Seven
EVERYDAY THEOLOGY IN THE iWORLD

[1] Dale Kuehne, *Sex and the iWorld: Rethinking Relationships beyond an Age of Individualisation, (Grand Rapids: Baker Academic, 2009), p.45.*

[2] Kuehne, pp.33–40.

[3] Steve Jobs, "Commencement address at Stanford University", *Stanford Report, June 15, 2005.*http://news.stanford.edu/news/2005/june15/jobs-061505.html (accessed May 7, 2012).

[4] Kevin Vanhoozer, "What is Everyday Theology? How and Why Christians Should Read Culture", in *Everyday Theology: How to Read Cultural Texts and Interpret Trends, edited by Kevin J. Vanhoozer, Charles A Anderson, and Michael J Sleasman, pp.15–60. (Grand Rapids: Baker Academic, 2007) p.16.*

[5] Vanhoozer, 2007, p.56.

[6] Vanhoozer, 2007, p.9.

[7] Vanhoozer, 2007, p.24.

[8] Darren Patrick, *Church Planter: The Man, The Message, The Mission, (Wheaton: Crossway, 2010) p.196.*

[9] Vanhoozer, 2007, p.19.

[10] Jean Twenge, *Generation Me: Why Today's Young Americans Are More Confident, Assertive, Entitled, and More Miserable Than Ever Before, (New York: Free Press, 2006) p.2.*

[11] Twenge, 2006, p.20.

[12] Arnett in Twenge, 2006, p.98.

[13] Twenge, 2006, p.2.

[14] Sennett in Brian Turner, "The Possibility of Primitiveness: Towards a Sociology of Body Marks in Cool Societies", *Body & Society 5, no.2-3, 1999, p.43*

[15] Zygmunt Bauman, in Adrian Franklin, "The Tourist Syndrome: an Interview with Zygmunt Bauman", *Tourist Studies 3, no.2, 2003, pp.207-208.*

[16] Franklin, 2003, p.209.

[17] Kuehne, 2009, p.69.

[18] See Frank Furedi, "The Silent Ascendancy of Therapeutic Culture in Britain", *Society 39, no.3, March/April, 2002, pp.16–24,* and *T J Jackson Lears, "From Salvation to Self-Actualisation: Advertising and the Therapeutic Roots of the Consumer Culture, 1880–1930",* in *The Culture of Consumption: Critical Essays in American History, 1880–1980, edited by Richard Wightman Fox and T J Jackson Lears, (New York: Pantheon Books,1983) pp.1–38.*

[19] Lears, 1983, paragraph 4.

[20] Paul Hiebert, *Transforming Worldviews: An Anthropological Understanding of How People Change, (Grand Rapids: Baker Academic, 2008) p.169.*

[21] See Lears, 1983.

[22] Hiebert, 2008, p.170.

[23] Anthony Giddens, *Modernity and Self-Identity: Self and Society in the Late Modern Age, (Stanford: Stanford University Press, 1991) p.5.*

[24] Christian Smith, *Soul-Searching: the Religious and Spiritual Lives of American Teenagers, (New York: Oxford University Press 2005).*

[25] Smith, 2005, p.151.

[26] Smith 2005, p.165.

[27] Smith 2005, p.148.

[28] Smith, 2005, p.154.

[29] John Berger, *Ways of Seeing*, (London: British Broadcasting Commission, 1972) p.131.

[30] Tania Lewis, "He Needs to Face His Fears with These Five Queers: Queer Eye for the Straight Guy, Makeover TV and the Lifestyle Expert", *Television & New Media 8, no.4, November 2007*, p.285.

[31] Frances Atikinson, "Through Thick and Thin", *The Sydney Morning Herald*, February 16, 2012. http://www.smh.com.au/entertainment/tv-and-radio/through-thick-and-thin-20120215-1t4nm.html (accessed May 7, 2012)

[32] Martin Seligman, *Flourish: A Visionary New Understanding of Happiness and Well-Being*, (North Sydney: Random House, 2011) pp.79–80.

[33] Twenge, 2006, p.109.

[34] Martin Seligman, *The Optimistic Child: A Revolutionary Approach to Raising Resilient Children*, (North Sydney: Random House, 1995) p.40.

[35] Jon-Jon Goulian, "Bret Easton Ellis, the Art of Fiction No.216", The Paris Review, no.200, Spring, 2002, http://www.theparisreview.org/interviews/6127/the-art-of-fiction-no-216-bret-easton-ellis (accessed May 7, 2012).

[36] Mark Sayers, *The Vertical Self: How Biblical Faith Can Help Us Discover Who We Are in an Age of Self-Obsession*, (Nashville: Thomas Nelson, 2010) p.17.

[37] Stanley Hauerwas, *A Community of Character: Towards a Constructive Christian Social Ethic*, (Indiana: University of Notre Dame Press, 1981) p.15.

[38] Franklin, 2003, p.209.

[39] Miroslav Volf, *Exclusion & Embrace: A Theological Exploration of Identity, Otherness and Reconciliation*, (Nashville, Abingdon Press, 1996) pp.38–43.

[40] Quoted in Debra Arca Mooney, "Almost Christian: An Interview with Kenda Creasy Dean", *Patheos, June 22, 2010*, http://www.patheos.com/Resources/Additional-Resources/Almost-Christian-Kenda-Creasy-Dean.html (accessed May 7, 2012)

[41] Timothy Keller, *Counterfeit Gods: When the Empty Promises of Money, Love and Power Let You Down*, (London: Hodder & Stoughton, 2009,) p.xxii.

[42] J K Rowling, "The Fringe Benefits of Failure and the Importance of the Imagination", Commencement Address at the Annual Meeting of the Harvard Alumni Association, *Harvard Magazine, June 5, 2008*. http://harvardmagazine.com/2008/06/the-fringe-benefits-failure-the-importance-imagination (accessed May 7, 2012.

[43] Rowling 2008: online

[44] Rosa Prince, "Forbes List: J K Rowling Fortune under Vanishing Spell", *The Telegraph, March 7, 2012*. http://www.telegraph.co.uk/culture/books/booknews/9129981/Forbes-list-JK-Rowling-fortune-under-vanishing-spell.html (accessed May 7, 2012.

[45] John Dickson, *Humilitas: A Key to Life, Love and Leadership*, (Grand Rapids: Zondervan, 2011) p.24.

Chapter Eight
PREACHING TO THE BIRDS?
THE MISSION OF THE CHURCH TO CREATION

[1] Lynn Townsend White, Jr, "The Historical Roots of Our Ecologic Crisis", *Science, Vol 155 (Number 3767), March 10, 1967*, pp. 1203–1207.

[2] N T Wright, *The New Testament and the People of God*, (Minneapolis: Fortress Press, 1992).

[3] Roger E Olson, *Reformed and Always Reforming: The Postconservative Approach to Evangelical Theology*, (Grand Rapids: Baker Academic, 2007).

[4] N T Wright. *Scripture and the Authority of God*, (SPCK: 2005).

[5] John H Walton. *The Lost World of Genesis One: Ancient Cosmology and the Origins Debate*, (IVP: 2009).

[6] In his chapter in John G Stackhouse (ed), *What Does It Mean to Be Saved? Broadening Evangelical Horizons of Salvation*, (Grand Rapids: Baker Academic, 2002).

[7] Tom Wright, *What St Paul Really Said*, (Lion Books: 1997).

[8] Wright, *What St Paul Really Said*.

[9] N T Wright. *Evil and the Justice of God*, (SPCK: 2006).

[10] Aleksandr Solzhenitsyn, *The Gulag Archipelago 1918–1956*, various editions.

[11] Wright. *Evil and the Justice of God*.

ENDNOTES

www.ingramcontent.com/pod-product-compliance
Lightning Source LLC
Chambersburg PA
CBHW072051290426
44110CB00014B/1640